nature babies

nature babies

natural knits and organic crafts for moms, babies, and a better world

tara jon manning

POTTER
CRAFT

new york

For Jack and Zane
and all the moms and babies, now and forever

Published in the United States by Potter Craft,
an imprint of the Crown Publishing Group,
a division of Random House, Inc., New York.
www.crownpublishing.com
www.pottercraft.com

POTTER CRAFT and CLARKSON N. POTTER
are trademarks, and POTTER and colophon are
registered trademarks of Random House, Inc.

Library of Congress
Cataloging-in-Publication Data:

Manning, Tara Jon, 1968-
   Nature babies : natural knits and
organic crafts for moms, babies,
and a better world / Tara Jon
Manning ; photographs by
Alexandra Grablewski. -- 1st ed.
   p. cm.
   ISBN-13: 978-0-307-33825-9 (hardcover)
   ISBN-10: 0-307-33825-8 (0-307-33825-8)
   1. Knitting. 2. Sewing. 3. Felting. I. Title.
   TT820.M28 2006
   746--dc22

                           2006023378

Printed in the United States of America

Design by Lauren Monchik and Jen Walter

Photography by Alexandra Grablewski

10 9 8 7 6 5 4 3 2

TABLE OF CONTENTS

introduction

What does baby need? Baby needs clothes, blankets, and toys. Baby needs hats and sweaters and bath-tubby time. Most of all, baby needs love and a safe, nurturing, natural environment in which to grow and thrive.

In Nature Babies, I offer you a collection of delightful and fun garments, accessory items, and gifts for baby, nursery, and mom. Each item is made by hand and comes from the heart. Through knitting, sewing, and working with felt, Nature Babies presents you and your baby with gifts and accessories that employ some of our Earth's loveliest materials and that fit the philosophies of a natural and holistic lifestyle. A step above a basic knitting or crafts book, Nature Babies beautifully combines the themes of natural and organic with utility to create unique items for moms (and moms-to-be), babies, and friends that are both treasures to make and comforts to enjoy.

I invite you to explore the environmentally low-impact benefits of using organic and natural materials to create things with your own hands. The handwork projects presented here in Nature Babies come with information about different types of fibers and their qualities, what makes them a good choice for babies and for the Earth, and how our choices, even in something as small as a craft project, can support sustainable manufacturing, making for a better world for all of us.

Perhaps most importantly, Nature Babies invites you to connect your heart, your mind, and your hands. This powerful combination of intention, vision, and creativity will allow you to explore the endless wealth of beauty inherent in all things. Bringing a new life into the world is an amazing, awe-inspiring act—perhaps the most creative of all endeavors. Let your creative force keep its momentum through the work of your hands.

Here almost every reader will find something familiar and something new. Maybe you're a knitter who's always wanted to make a charming little doll—so now you are going to sew. Or perhaps you've always sewn but have been intrigued by the fun new trends in felt—here's your opportunity. Through all kinds of handwork and their interrelated skills, we can create items of unique beauty—not unlike our own little babies. Make them special, inspirational, and imaginative garments and toys that they will play with and cherish for years, if not generations.

As we make these crafts to give our little ones, we demonstrate and instill in them a respect for simplicity and beauty, following the maxim "Live simply so others may simply live." With these garments and playthings, we can teach the next generation that less is more and that we can make smart choices about what we use and how we use it. As we care for and nourish our babies, we can likewise nourish their world through the good works of our hands.

projects to knit

Knitting is a classic craft often used to welcome new babies. A new mom can fashion lovely items to provide warmth for her loved ones and to decorate the nursery. In turn, the act of knitting can provide her with comfort. In this chapter, you will find projects to knit with beautiful natural and organic yarns. Take advantage of the full range of natural fibers, from lusciously soft organic cotton to sturdy hemp and naturally processed color-grown yarns. In choosing these fibers, we lessen the impact of the production processes on the Earth and support the production and consumption of low-impact and organically produced goods. The projects are quick and easy to knit—a novice knitter will have fun learning lots of new techniques, while a seasoned knitter will enjoy the benefits of a few time-saving tricks and deluxe fiber blends.

hemp stroller tote

This handy tote is simply a rectangular bag, knit in openwork on one side and solid garter stitch on the other. It can be carried to the market or attached to the handle of your stroller with knitted tabs. Made from natural hemp-blend yarn, this bag will be helpful even after baby is grown. Make it as a gift to fill with shower goodies or indulgences just for mom, then let it go back to work as a market bag or tote once baby has outgrown the stroller.

FINISHED MEASUREMENTS: APPROXIMATELY 16" (40.5CM) DEEP X 14" (36CM) WIDE

yarn

2 skeins of EnviroTextiles Hemp
   Yarn; (4oz[113g]/ 250yd[228m]
   55% hemp, 45% wool) in Natural

needles

Size 10 (6mm), or size to obtain
   gauge
Size 8 (5mm) for strap

notions

Two ½" (1.25cm) buttons
Measuring tape
Yarn needle
Scissors
Stitch holders
Stitch markers (optional)
Crochet hook (optional)

gauge

12½ stitches and 28 rows =
   4" (10cm) in garter stitch
Check the gauge before you begin.

NOTE *Purse stitch is knit as follows: (Multiple of 2 stitches + 2)*
Row 1: K1, *yo, p2tog; rep from * across to last st, end k1.
Repeat Row 1 for purse stitch.

front

Loosely cast on 46 stitches. Work in garter stitch for 12 rows/6 ridges.

Set pattern for front openwork pattern as follows, placing markers (pm) between panels if desired:

Work 6 stitches in garter stitch, pm, work 34 stitches in purse stitch, pm, work 6 stitches in garter stitch.

Continue to work even in pattern until piece measures 14½" (36.8cm), ending with a WS row. Then work 12 rows/6 ridges in garter stitch. Mark this point with a scrap of contrasting yarn (at lower edge).

back

Continue to work even in garter stitch for 16" (40.5cm) more, or until the back measures same as the front when piece is folded at contrasting yarn marker. Loosely bind off all stitches.

finishing

With the piece folded at the contrasting yarn marker, sew side seams. Remove marker.

strap

With smaller needles, cast on 10 stitches. Work even in garter stitch until strap measures approximately 28" (71cm), or desired length. Bind off all stitches. Sew the strap into place at side seams.

stroller tabs (make two)

With smaller needles, cast on 7 stitches. Work even in stockinette stitch for 4" (10cm), ending with a WS row.

Next row make buttonhole: K3, YO, k2tog, k3. Continue in stockinette stitch for 4 rows more. Bind off all stitches.

Attach tabs Attach end without buttonhole to WS of the front of the bag, approximately 2" (5cm) in from side seam. Secure the tab to the bag by sewing it securely in the garter stitch section at the top of the bag. Repeat for second tab. Sew buttons securely to back of bag, approximately 1" (2.5cm) down from top opening, to correspond with the tab placement. Weave in ends.

THE HISTORY OF HEMP

Hemp production in the United States was all but eliminated in the 1930s, when the government refused to distinguish industrial hemp from marijuana plants. Early legislation heavily taxed hemp production, and subsequent laws banned it altogether. The brief exception was during World War II, when the U.S. Department of Agriculture led the "Hemp for Victory" campaign to encourage farmers to grow hemp in support of the war effort. Once the war ended, hemp production did too.

About Hemp

Grown from seed, hemp is an annual plant, similar to flax, jute, and ramie. Known as bast fiber plants, or plants that produce long fibers within their stems, this entire family of plants creates fibers with exceptional strength, durability, and absorbency. The hemp plant has been cultivated all over the world since the dawn of recorded time. Hemp oil is one of the richest known sources of polyunsaturated essential fatty acids, which give the plant its antimicrobial and antifungal properties. For centuries, the plant's strong fibers have been used to make linenlike fabrics, paper, rope, and heavy sailcloth. It was grown in abundance in the American colonies; in fact, the Declaration of Independence may have been drafted on hemp paper.

Industrial hemp produces a wide variety of important and useful products, and its cultivation and manufacturing processes are environmentally friendly. Hemp is naturally pest resistant, meaning hemp crops require minimal or only natural predatory pest control. Because the plants can be grown in tightly spaced arrangements, weeds are naturally inhibited, minimizing or eliminating the use of herbicides. When made into paper, hemp can be bleached through a hydrogen peroxide method, reducing the release of harmful chlorine components into the ecosystem.

The industrial hemp plant is classified as *Cannabis sativa*, a species comprising hundreds of varieties, including the marijuana plant. While the untrained eye may see some similarity between industrial hemp and marijuana, the two are in fact very different. Most significantly, the industrial hemp plant contains mere trace amounts of tetrahydrocannabinol, or THC, the agent that makes marijuana a psychoactive drug.

Now that industrial hemp production is being revived in other parts of the world, ecologically minded consumers are becoming aware of the plant's many benefits to the Earth's ecology. How long will it be before industrial hemp is once again a staple crop in North America?

hugs and kisses
hoodie sweater

Babies rejoice! Here is an ingenious and classic hooded sweater that doesn't have to be pulled over baby's head! This is an updated version of the back-zip design, featuring roomy shaping, modern details at the cuff and bottom edges, and a beautiful, simple-to-knit cable design running up the center front. The cable forms an X-and-O shape that reminds me of the written shorthand for "hugs and kisses"—something with which we cannot help but cover our babies.

SIZES: 6–9 (12–18, 24) MONTHS (SHOWN IN SIZE 24 MONTHS)
CIRCUMFERENCE AT UNDERARM: 21 (25, 29)"[53 (64, 73)CM]
TOTAL LENGTH: 12 (14, 15)"/30.5 (36, 38)CM • SLEEVE LENGTH: 7 (10, 11)"[18 (25, 28)CM]

yarn

3 (3, 4) skeins of Mostly Merino Worsted Weight 77% merino wool, 23% mohair; (2oz[58g]/125yd[115m]) in Natural Gray

needles

Size 8 (5mm), or size to obtain gauge
Size 7 (4.5mm)
Spare needle for three-needle bind-off

notions

Measuring tape
Yarn needle
Scissors
20 (22, 24)" [51 (56, 61)cm] all-purpose or sportswear zipper in coordinating color
Hand sewing needle and thread in coordinating color
Stitch markers (optional)
Size H/8 (5mm) crochet hook (optional)
Stitch holders
Straight pins

gauge

16 stitches and 24 rows = 4" (10cm) in stockinette stitch, using size 8 (5mm) needles
Check the gauge before you begin.

techniques

Three-needle bind-off (see page 139)

NOTE *Allow the lower edges of the garment to roll naturally when measuring lengths.*

ABOUT THE YARN

The yarn used for this project is an undyed wool blend from Vermont-based Mostly Merino, owned and operated by Margaret Klein Wilson. Margaret produces batches of fiber from the wool of her small flock, which is then blended and "Greenspun" at nearby Green Mountain Spinnery. The spinnery uses vegetable-based soaps and oils, rather than the petroleum-based products standard in the textile industry, and does not use chemicals to treat the yarn.

front

NOTE *It is helpful to place a marker each side of cable panel on front.*

With smaller needles, cast on 44 (52, 60) stitches.

Work for 7 rows in stockinette stitch for lower edge roll, ending with a WS row.

Increase Row (RS): K18 (22, 26), make 1, k2, make 1, k4, make 1, k2, make 1, k18 (22, 26)—48 (56, 64) stitches.

Set Pattern (WS): Change to larger needles; p18 (22, 26), k2, p8, k2, p18 (22, 26).

(RS) K18 (22, 26), place a marker (pm); work 12 stitches from XO Cable Chart; pm, k18 (22, 26).

Continue to work in pattern, working from chart over center 12 stitches, until piece measures 6 (7, 8)" [15 (17.8, 20.3cm] from base of rolled edge, ending with a WS row.

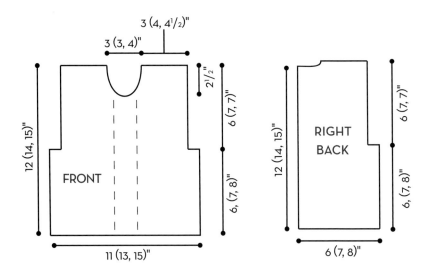

Shape armholes: Bind off 2 (2, 3) stitches at the beginning of the next 2 rows—44 (52, 58) stitches remain.

Continue to work in pattern until piece measures 9½ (11½ , 12½)"[24 (29, 31)cm] from base of rolled edge, ending with a WS row.

Shape front neck: (RS) Work 16 (20, 22) stitches, join a second skein of yarn, bind off the center 12 (12, 14) stitches, work 16 (20, 22) stitches. Working both sides at the same time, at each neck edge, bind off 1 stitch every other row 4 times—12 (16, 18) stitches remain for each shoulder.

Continue to work even until piece measures 12 (14, 15)"[30 (36, 38)cm] from base of rolled edge. Place remaining stitches for each shoulder on separate stitch holders.

back (right side)
With smaller needles, cast on 24 (28, 32) stitches.

Work 7 rows in stockinette stitch for lower rolled edge, ending with a WS row.

Change to larger needles and continue to work even in stockinette stitch until piece measures 6 (7, 8)"[15 (18, 20)cm] from base of rolled edge, ending with a WS row.

Shape armhole: (RS) At the beginning of this row (armhole edge), bind off 2 (2, 3) stitches, work to end—22 (26, 29) stitches remain.

Continue to work even until piece measures 11³/₄ (13³/₄, 14³/₄)"[29.8 (34.9, 37.5)cm] from base of rolled edge, ending with a right side row.

Shape back neck: (WS) At the beginning of this row (neck edge), bind off 10 (10, 11) stitches, work remaining 12 (16, 18) stitches for shoulder. Continue to work even in stockinette stitch until piece measures 12 (14, 15)"[30 (36, 38)cm] from base of rolled edge. Place shoulder stitches on a stitch holder.

back (left side)
Work as for right back, reversing all shaping.

In other words, work even in stockinette stitch until piece measures 6 (7, 8)"[15 (18, 20)cm] from base of rolled edge, ending with a right side row.

Shape armhole as for the right back at the beginning of next (WS) row.

Continue to work even until piece measures 11³/₄ (13³/₄, 14³/₄)"[29.8 (34.9, 37.5)cm] from base of rolled edge, ending with a WS row.

Shape neck as for the right back at the beginning of the next (RS) row.

Complete piece as for the right back.

shoulders
With right sides together, join shoulders using the three-needle bind-off method.

sleeves (make 2)
With right side of sweater facing, using the larger needles (and a crochet hook to assist), pick up evenly and knit 48 (56, 56) stitches around the armhole, beginning and ending at the armhole notches (where the shaping begins).

Begin working in stockinette stitch; work even for 5 (5, 7) rows.

Shape sleeve: Decrease 1 stitch each side this row, then every 3 (4, 4) rows 11 (7, 13) times, every 0 (3, 0) rows 0 (6, 0) times—24 (28, 28) stitches remain. Continue to work even until sleeve measures 7 (9, 11)"[18 (23, 28)cm] from the shoulder beginning.

Change to smaller needles; work 7 rows in stockinette stitch for rolled edge.

Loosely bind off all stitches.

Repeat for second sleeve.

hood

With larger needles, loosely cast on 31 (35, 39) stitches.

Work even in stockinette stitch until hood measures 14 (16, 18)"[36 (41, 46)cm], or desired height of hood (measured from shoulder to shoulder).

Loosely bind off all stitches.

finishing

Sew the underarm/sleeve seams.

Weave in all ends.

Lightly steam block, only if necessary.

Attach hood: With right sides together, pin the hood to the neck, lining up the center back and back edges of the hood, and with the front edges of hood overlapped at center front cable; then pin the remaining seam, easing the hood to fit, and distributing the extra fullness across the back neck to make the hood a bit fuller. Carefully and neatly sew the edges of the hood to the neck edges.

XO Cable Chart
12 stitches; 16-row repeat

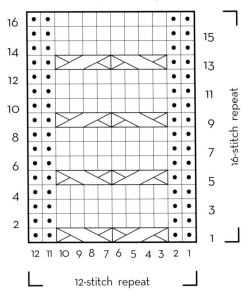

16-stitch repeat

12-stitch repeat

KEY

☐ Knit on right side, purl on wrong side.

▪ Purl on right side, knit on wrong side.

▨ Slip 2 stitches to cable needle, hold to front, knit 2, knit 2 from cable needle.

▨ Slip 2 stitches to cable needle, hold to back, knit 2, knit 2 from cable needle.

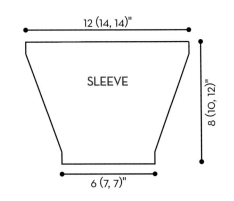

12 (14, 14)"

SLEEVE

8 (10, 12)"

6 (7, 7)"

Apply zipper: Pin closed zipper down the center back edges, with the bottom closed end of zipper at the top of the hood, and any extra length at the lower edge. When zipper is closed, pull tab is at the lower edge of the sweater. After pinning, open zipper to make sewing easier.

Using sewing needle and matching thread, beginning at the top of the hood on each side and working toward lower edge, baste zipper into place, stopping 2" (5cm) from the lower edge. Close zipper and adjust basting if necessary.

Open zipper; beginning at the top of the hood on each side and working toward lower edge, sew zipper in place, stopping 2" (5cm) from lower edge. Fold excess zipper to WS, aligning end of zipper approximately 1" (2.5cm) above base of roll. (Note: If there is more than an inch of extra length, cut excess, leaving approximately 1" [2.5cm] to fold under.) With the excess folded between the zipper and the sweater, sew remainder of zipper in place, being sure to catch both layers if excess zipper is folded back.

cables-and-checkers aran sweater

This richly cabled sweater uses the magic of color-grown cotton yarns. Using the intarsia technique, classic Aran stitch patterns are combined with color knit sections to juxtapose the subtle colors of the yarn and the rich texture of cable stitches. A great project for a knitter who wants to play around with both texture and color, this one is a beauty!

SIZES: TO FIT 6–9 (12–18, 24) MONTHS (SHOWN IN SIZE 24 MONTHS)
CIRCUMFERENCE AT UNDERARM: 24 (26, 28)"[61 (66, 71)CM]
TOTAL LENGTH: 12 (14, 16)"[30 (36, 41)CM]

yarn

1 ball of Blue Sky Organic Cotton
(100% organic color-grown
cotton; 35oz[110g]/ 150yd[137m])
in #81 Sand (MC), and
1 ball each in #83 Sage (CC1) and
#82 Nut (CC2)

NOTE *This color-grown cotton yarn is naturally pigmented and processed without dyes or chemicals.*

needles

Size 8 (5mm), or size to obtain
gauge
Size 7 (4.5mm) single-point
Double-pointed needles
Spare needle (for three-needle
bind-off)

notions

Cable needle
Size G/6 (4mm) crochet hook
Stitch holders
Stitch markers (optional)

gauge

16 stitches and 22 rows = 4"/10cm in
seed stitch
Check the gauge before you begin.

techniques

intarsia (see page 138), three-
needle bind-off (see page 139)

back

With smaller needles and MC, cast on 48 (52, 56) stitches.

Work 7 rows in stockinette stitch for rolled edge, ending with a WS row.

Change to k2/p2 rib; work 6 rows, ending with a WS row.

Color Ridges: Change to larger needles and work 26 rows from Color Ridge Chart (see page 24), ending with a WS row.

Next row (RS): Join MC, knit 1 row.

Following row (WS): Set pattern, placing markers (pm) between stitch panels if desired, as follows: Work [p1, k1] 2 (3, 4) times, p1 (seed stitch); k5 (Bobble panel); p4 Cable; k2, p4, k2, p4, k2, p4, k2 (center Lattice panel); p4 (Cable), k5 (Bobble panel); p1, [k1, p1] 2 (3, 4) times (in seed stitch).

(RS) Beginning Row 1 of Charts A,

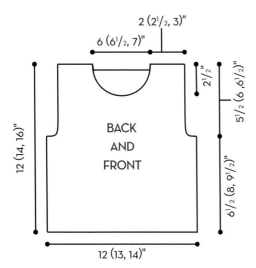

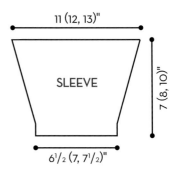

BACK AND FRONT

SLEEVE

2 (2½, 3)"

6 (6½, 7)"

2½"

5½ (6, 6½)"

12 (14, 16)"

6½ (8, 9½)"

12 (13, 14)"

11 (12, 13)"

7 (8, 10)"

6½ (7, 7½)"

B, C, and D, work 5 (7, 9) stitches from Chart A, 5 stitches from Chart B, 4 stitches from Chart C, 20 stitches from Chart D, 4 stitches from Chart E, 5 stitches from Chart B, and 5 (7, 9) stitches from Chart A.

Continue to work as set, following charts, until piece measures 6½ (8, 9½)"[16½ (20, 24)cm] from cast-on edge, ending with a WS row.

Shape armholes: Bind off 2 stitches at beginning of next two rows—44 (48, 52) stitches remain.
Continue to work even as set until piece measures 11½ (13½, 15½)"[29 (34, 39)cm] from cast-on edge.

Shape back neck: Work 8 (10, 12) stitches, join a second ball of yarn, bind off center 28 stitches, work to end—8 (10, 12) stitches remain each shoulder. Working both side at the same time, continue to work even on remaining stitches until total length measures 12 (14, 16)"[30 (36, 41)cm] from cast-on edge. Place shoulder stitches on holders.

front

Work as for the back until piece measures 9½ (11½, 13½)"[24 (29, 34)cm]—44 (48, 52) stitches remain.

Shape front neck: Work 12 (14, 16) stitches, join a second ball of yarn, bind off center 20 stitches, work to end. Working both sides at the same time, at each neck edge, decrease 1 stitch each side every other row 4 times—8 (10, 12) stitches remain each shoulder. Continue to work even on remaining stitches until piece measures same as back to shoulders. Place shoulder stitches on holders.

Join shoulders: With right sides facing, join shoulders using the three-needle bind-off technique. Check to be sure you are matching the right front shoulder to the right back shoulder and the left front shoulder to the left back shoulder. The bind-off ridge is now on the WS of the garment.

sleeves

With RS facing, using larger needles and crochet hook to assist if desired, evenly pick up 44 (48, 52) stitches between armhole notches. Work in seed stitch for 2 (3, 4)"[5 (7.5, 10)cm], then work 26 rows of Color Ridge Chart, and AT THE SAME TIME, beg sleeve shaping as follows: decrease 1 stitch each side every fourth row 9 (10, 11) times—26 (28, 30) stitches remain. When chart is completed and all decreases have been worked, change to smaller needles and MC, and work 1 row in stockinette stitch. Change to k2/p2 rib for approximately 1" (2.5cm), or until sleeve measures 7 (8, 10)"[18 (20, 25)cm]. Change to stockinette stitch; work even for 7 rows or desired length of rolled edge. Loosely bind off all stitches. Repeat for second sleeve.

finishing

Weave in all ends.

Sew underarm/side seams.

neck edge

Beginning at left shoulder seam, using MC and double-pointed needles, evenly pick up 10 stitches along left front edge, 16 stitches across center front, 10 stitches up right front edge, 24 stitches across back. Place a marker if desired to make beginning of round. Working in the round, work 1" (2.5cm) in k2/p2 rib, then change to stockinette stitch and work 7 rows or desired length of rolled edge. Loosely bind off all stitches. Weave in ends.

Multi-tone Charts

Color Ridge Chart

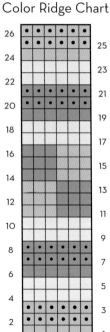

CHART A
SEED STITCH
2 STITCH; 2=ROW REPEAT

CHART B
BOBBLE
5 STITCHES; 4=ROW REPEAT

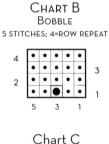

Chart C
CABLE 1
4 STITCHES; 4=ROW REPEAT

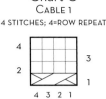

CHART D
LATTICE
20 STITCHES; 8-ROW REPEAT

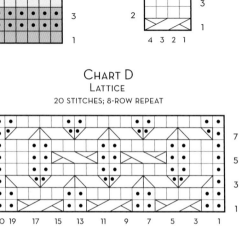

Key

- ☐ Knit on RS, purl on WS
- • Purl on RS, knit on WS
- ☐ Color A: Sand (MC)
- ■ Color B: Rust
- ▨ Color C: Sage
- ⬤ Bobble: [K1 through the back loop, purl 1, K1 through the back loop, purl 1] into the next stitch, to make 4 stitches in one; pass the first 3 stitches on the right-hand needle over the 4th stitch to return the count to 1 stitch.

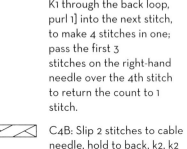

C4B: Slip 2 stitches to cable needle, hold to back, k2, k2 from the cable needle.

C4F: Slip two stitches to cable needle, hold to front, k2, k2 from the cable needle.

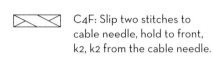

C3Bp: Slip 1 stitch to cable needle, hold to back, k2, p1 from cable needle.

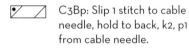

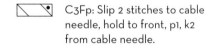

C3Fp: Slip 2 stitches to cable needle, hold to front, p1, k2 from cable needle.

About Color-Grown Cotton

When we think of cotton, we often think of bright, fresh white cloth. But the origins of cotton are much more colorful—literally. As many as 5,000 years ago, the native peoples of Peru cultivated cotton in the most exciting range of color and quality, with a long fiber that made it superb for spinning into yarn.

Throughout history, colored cotton has been grown all over the world. Naturally pigmented, this color-grown cotton is found in a wide range of colors, including browns, mauves, greens, and shades of cream. What has recently become known as color-grown cotton was in fact grown in several locations around the world right up until the industrial revolution, when machinery and chemical dyes made it less expensive to produce colored cotton with dyes.

Contemporary consumers of natural products have rediscovered color-grown cotton and welcomed it with open arms. In Peru, farmers are once again growing color cotton using native agricultural techniques and no pesticides, resulting in a certified organic yarn. Because the yarn also requires no chemical dyes, it is a truly low process/low impact (not to mention beautiful) product. Perhaps best of all, the natural pigments within the color-grown cotton fiber intensify with exposure to warmth. As the fabrics they make are worn and washed, they deepen and transform, reminding us of both their organic properties and their rich history.

greenspun stripes sweater and knickers set

This matching sweater and darling knickers set plays on the theme of the vintage baby set, with a thoroughly modern and cheerful attitude. Stripes of stockinette and reverse stockinette stitch create a fun texture, enhanced by the pastel colors of the supersoft organic "Greenspun" yarns—fiber blends that can be worn all year. Only the best for baby! This set is sure to be an all-time favorite and the hit gift of any baby shower.

greenspun stripes sweater

SWEATER SIZES: 6–9 (12–18, 24) MONTHS (SHOWN IN SIZE 12 MONTHS)
SWEATER CIRCUMFERENCE AT UNDERARM: $23^{1}/_{2}$ (25, 28)"[59 (64, 71)CM] (WHEN BUTTONED)
SWEATER LENGTH: 10 (11, 12)"[25 (28, 30)CM]
SWEATER SLEEVE LENGTH: 7 (9, 10)"[18 (23, 25)CM]

yarn

2 skeins of Green Mountain Spinnery Cotton Comfort (fine wool, 20% organic cotton; 2oz[57g]/180yd[166m]) in Bluelle (MC) and 1 skein each in Maize (CC1), Pink Lilac (CC2), and Mint (CC3), or color combinations of choice

NOTE *If making the set, one skein of each CC should be sufficient yardage for both pieces for the smallest size*

needles

Size 6 (4mm), or size to obtain gauge
Size 5 (3.75mm)

notions

Measuring tape
Yarn needle
Scissors
Spare needle (for three-needle bind-off)
Stitch holders
Small crochet hook
5 (5, 6) $^{1}/_{2}$" (1.3cm) buttons

gauge

20 stitches and 28 rows = 4" (10cm) in stockinette stitch
Check the gauge before you begin.

techniques

Three-needle bind-off (see page 139)

TIPS *The body of the sweater is worked in one piece to the underarm and then separated for back and front. You may choose to use circular needles for this pattern, even though you will not be working in the round. Working straight on circular needles makes it easier to accommodate the number of stitches needed for the body of this sweater. Also, to minimize the number of yarn ends you have to weave in later, don't cut the yarn after you finish working a colored stripe. Instead, leave yarns of different colors attached and loosely strand them up the side of your work until you need the new color.*

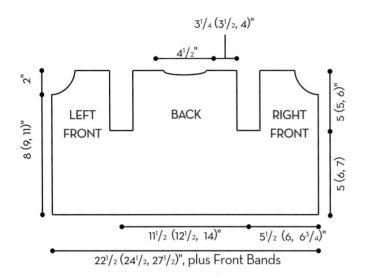

3¼ (3½, 4)"

4½"

LEFT FRONT

BACK

RIGHT FRONT

2"

8 (9, 11)"

5 (5, 6)"

5 (6, 7)"

11½ (12½, 14)"

5½ (6, 6¾)"

22½ (24½, 27½)", plus Front Bands

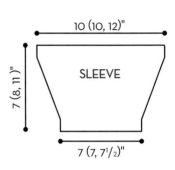

10 (10, 12)"

SLEEVE

7 (8, 11)"

7 (7, 7½)"

body

With smaller needles and MC, loosely cast on 114 (122, 138) stitches. Work in garter stitch for 10 rows/5 ridges, ending with a WS row. Change to larger needle and begin working Stripe pattern from chart (see page 32). Continue to work even as set until piece measures 5 (6, 7)"[13 (15, 18)cm] from the beginning, ending with a WS row (Row 8 or 18 of stripe pattern).

Shape underarms: (RS) Continuing in stripe pattern, work 26 (27, 30) stitches for the right front; bind off 4 (6, 8) stitches for underarm; work 54 (56, 62) stitches for the back; bind off 4 (6, 8) stitches for underarm; work remaining 26 (27, 30) stitches for the left front. Place stitches for the back and right front on holders.

left front

Working on left front stitches only, work even in stripe pattern as set until piece measures 8 (9, 11)"[20 (23, 28)cm] from beginning, ending with a right side row.

Shape neck: (WS) At the neck edge (center front), bind off 6 stitches, work to end. Work 1 row even.

Then at neck edge, decrease 1 stitch every other row 4 times—16 (17, 20) stitches remain for shoulder. Continuing in stripe pattern, work even until piece measures 10 (11, 13)"[25 (28, 33)cm] from the beginning. Place left shoulder 16 (17, 20) stitches on a stitch holder.

right front

With WS facing, continuing in stripe pattern as set, rejoin yarn at underarm, ready to work a WS row. Work as for the left front, reversing shaping.

In other words, work neck shaping at the beginning of right side rows when piece measures the same length as the left front to beginning of neck shaping.

back

With WS facing, continuing in stripe pattern as set, rejoin yarn at underarm, ready to work a WS row. Work even until piece measures 9¾ (10¾, 12¾)"[25 (27, 32)cm] from the beginning, ending with a WS row.

Shape neck: (RS) Work 16 (17, 20) stitches for right shoulder; join a second skein of yarn and bind off center 22 stitches for neck; work across to end. Working both sides at the same time, work even until piece measures 10 (11, 13)"[25 (28, 32)cm] from the beginning. Place remaining shoulder stitches on separate stitch holders.

Join shoulders: With right sides facing, join shoulders using the three-needle bind-off method.

sleeves (make two)

With smaller needles and MC, loosely cast on 35 (35, 37) stitches. Work in garter stitch for 10 rows/5 ridges, ending with a WS row. Change to larger needle and beginning Row 1 of chart, work even in stripe pattern from chart for 2 (4, 4) rows.

Shape sleeves: Continuing in stripe pattern as set, increase 1 stitch each side this row, then every 6 (7, 7) rows 7 (7, 11) times—51 (51, 61) stitches. Work even as set until sleeve measures 7 (10, 11)"[18 (25, 28)cm] from the beginning, ending with a right side row (Row 9 or 17 of stripe pattern).
Bind off all stitches loosely.

finishing

Sew the sleeves into the armhole openings; sew sleeve seams.

neck band

With RS facing, beginning at right front neck edge, using smaller needles and MC, pick up and knit 20 stitches along right front edge; 22 stitches across back neck, and 20 stitches along neck shaping to left front edge—62 stitches. Work in garter stitch for 6 rows, ending with a right side row. Bind off all stitches loosely on next (WS) row.

front bands

NOTE *Work buttonholes on right front for girls, on left front for boys/unisex.*

Button band: With RS facing, smaller needles and MC, pick up and knit 40 (45, 55) stitches along center front edge. Work in garter stitch for 6 rows, ending with a right side row. Bind off all stitches loosely on next (WS) row.

Buttonhole band: Place markers along front edge for button holes, the first centered in the garter stitch band at lower edge, the last centered on neck band, the remaining 3 (3, 4) evenly spaced between.

Work as for button band, working buttonholes opposite markers using yarn-over buttonhole technique [YO, k2tog].

Weave in all ends.

Lightly steam block if necessary.

Securely sew buttons in place opposite buttonholes.

greenspun stripes knickers

SIZES: 6–12 (24) MONTHS
CIRCUMFERENCE AT WAISTBAND: 21 (23)"[53.3 (58.4)CM]
INSEAM: 4 (6)"[10 (15)CM]
LEG LENGTH: 10 (12)"[25 (30)CM]

yarn

1 skein of Green Mountain Spinnery Cotton Comfort (80% fine wool, 20% organic cotton; 2oz[57g]/ 180yd[166m]) in Bluet (MC) and one skein each in Maize (CC1), Pink Lilac (CC2), and Mint (CC 3), or color combinations of choice

NOTE *If making the set, one skein of each CC should be sufficient yardage for both pieces for the smallest size.*

needles

Size 6 (4mm), or size to obtain gauge
Size 5 (3.75mm) for trim

notions

Measuring tape
Yarn needle
Scissors

gauge

20 stitches and 28 rows = 4" (10cm) in stockinette stitch
Check the gauge before you begin.

techniques

Three-needle bind-off (see page 139)

knickers (make 2)

With smaller needles and MC, loosely cast on 50 (54) stitches. Work even in garter stitch for 6 ridges (12 rows). Change to larger needle and begin working stripe pattern from chart (see below). Work even until piece measures 4 (6)"[10 (15)cm] from cast-on. Cast on 4 (5) stitches at the beginning of the next two rows.

Continue to work as established in stripe pattern from chart until total length measures 10 (12)"[25 (30)cm]. Work to the end of current stripe in sequence, evenly decreasing 4 (6) stitches along last WS row.

Next Row:

(RS) change to smaller needles and MC, and work even in 1/1 ribbing for 3" (7.6cm), or desired length of waistband. Loosely bind off all stitches.

finishing

Weave in all ends.

Sew pieces together: With MC, sew together the 2 pieces at the center front and center back from top of waistband (at bind-off) to base of crotch (where stitches each side were cast on).

Sew inseam: With MC, sew inseam, beginning at inside lower edge of right side and ending at inside lower edge of left side.

Weave in ends.

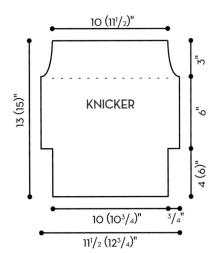

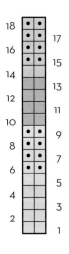

KEY

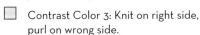 Contrast Color 1: Knit on right side, purl on wrong side.

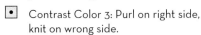 Contrast Color 3: Knit on right side, purl on wrong side.

Contrast Color 3: Purl on right side, knit on wrong side.

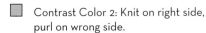 Contrast Color 2: Knit on right side, purl on wrong side.

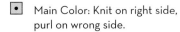 Main Color: Knit on right side, purl on wrong side.

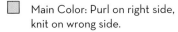 Main Color: Purl on right side, knit on wrong side.

cabled greenspun beanie

This snuggly cabled cap is knit flat. Once all the shaping is complete, the seam is sewn, joining the two outside seed stitch panels—one of the easiest and most invisible stitches to sew up. The soft "Greenspun" blend of fine wool and organic cotton makes for a lightweight, all-weather cap. The generous styling will ensure your little nature baby is warm and comfy!

SIZES: 6–12 (12–24) MONTHS (SHOWN IN SIZE 12-24 MONTHS)
CIRCUMFERENCE: 16 (18)"[41 (46)CM]

yarn
1 skein of Green Mountain
    Spinnery Cotton Comfort (80%
    fine wool, 20% organic cotton;
    2oz[57g]/180yd[166m]) in Natural

NOTE Two hats can be made from
1 skein of yarn.

needles
Size 6 (4mm), or size to obtain
    gauge

notions
Measuring tape
Yarn needle
Scissors
Cable needle
Stitch markers (optional)

gauge
20 stitches and 36 rows = 4" (10cm)
    in seed stitch
Check the gauge before you begin.

techniques
Decrease (see page 137)

TIPS *Since this project is small, it is the ideal opportunity to try out turning a cable. You may even surprise yourself with how easy it is. Seed stitch is used between cables.*

beanie
Loosely cast on 75 (95) stitches. Work for 15 rows in garter stitch, evenly increasing 5 stitches across the last (WS) row—80 (100) stitches. You will have 8 garter ridges when you are done.

Establish pattern: Row 1 (RS): Begin working from Cable Chart (see page 36) as follows: * 4 stitches in seed stitch, 12 stitches for cable, 4 stitches in seed stitch; repeat from * across, working 20-stitch repeat 4 (5) times.

Work even from chart, repeating Rows 1–6 until total length measures approximately 4 (5)"[10 (13)cm], ending with Row 2 (WS) of Cable Chart as shown.

Decrease for crown (see chart on page 36):
Row 1: * Work 3 stitches in seed stitch (one stitch before knit stitch of cable panel), k2tog (knit stitch from cable panel together with adjacent seed stitch), work next 10 stitches of cable panel, SSK knit stitch from cable panel with adjacent seed stitch); repeat from * across row—72 (90) stitches remain.

Row 2: Work across the row, knitting the knit stitches and purling the purl stitches of the cable panels as they face you, and keeping in sequence of seed stitch as set.

Repeat Rows 1 and 2 a total of 4 times—8 rows worked; 48 (60) stitches remain.

Next row (RS): Work across remaining stitches, turning cables as per Row 5 of chart.

Purl one row.

Continue shaping: * K1, k2tog; repeat from * across the row—32 (40) stitches remain.

Next row (WS): Purl across the row.

(RS) K2tog across row—16 (20) stitches remain.

Next row (WS): Purl across the row.

Cut yarn, leaving 12–18" (30–46cm) tail, draw through remaining stitches, gather tightly, fasten securely, and sew seam. Weave in ends.

GS CABLE HAT
Chart

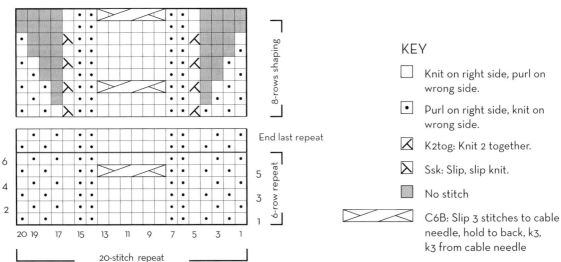

Complete shaping per instructions

8-rows shaping

End last repeat

6-row repeat

20-stitch repeat

KEY

☐ Knit on right side, purl on wrong side.

• Purl on right side, knit on wrong side.

⊼ K2tog: Knit 2 together.

⊠ Ssk: Slip, slip knit.

▨ No stitch

⟆ C6B: Slip 3 stitches to cable needle, hold to back, k3, k3 from cable needle

About Organics

"Organic" refers to the way in which agricultural products, including foodstuff and fiber, are grown and processed. Organic production strives to maintain and replenish soil fertility without the use of toxic pesticides, herbicides, or fertilizers. Organic products are minimally processed without the addition of artificial ingredients or components. To be certified as organic, a product must meet a third-party standard or state certification.

Organic farming supports small and rural farms, in some cases reviving them and returning livelihood to family farms. Organic producers use alternative methods of pest control such as insect predators, barriers, and hand-removal of pests from crops. The organic farmer's elimination of polluting and harmful chemicals from the growth and production cycle of crops prevents contamination of soil, air, and water resources. Not only do we end up with a superior product through organic production, but we also end up with a cleaner Earth and a more sustainable way of living on it.

Organic production enhances the ecological balance of nature and has its eye on the prize of a sustainable future for all of us. In the short run, your purchase and use of organic products allows you to put pure ingredients in and on you and your baby. You can be assured that certified organic fibers, yarns, and fabrics are minimally processed, often with no dyes at all. These materials are perfect for baby's new and tender skin—the body's largest organ.

In the long run, your choice to spend your money on an organic product helps the industry solidify, thrive, and grow. Choosing organically produced goods will improve and heal our ecosystem, leading us back toward a more sustainable way of living in harmony with the Earth. In the past few decades, we have seen a significant increase in the production and consumption of organic goods. Let's keep that momentum, making a cleaner and safer world for our children.

organic cotton topper

This playful hat is a great beginner project. Similar to the Cables-and-Checkers Aran Sweater on page 20, the hat can be made using leftover yarn from the sweater.

SIZES: 6–12 (12–24) MONTHS (SHOWN IN SIZE 12–24 MONTHS)
CIRCUMFERENCE: 16 (18)"[41 (46)CM]

yarn

1 skein of Blue Sky Alpacas Organic Cotton (100% organic cotton; 3¹/₂oz[110g]/150yd[137m]) in #81 Sand (MC) and small amounts (approximately 10yd[91.5m] in #83 Sage (CC1) and #82 Nut (CC2)

needles

Size 8 (5mm) circular needles, 16" (40cm) long
Set of four size 8 (5mm) double-pointed needles (DPN), or size to obtain gauge

notions

Measuring tape
Yarn needle
Scissors
Stitch marker

gauge

18 stitches and 24 rows = 4" (10cm) in stockinette stitch
Check the gauge before you begin.

Color Ridge Chart

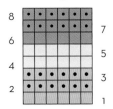

KEY

☐ Knit on right side, purl on wrong side

☒ Purl on right side, knit on wrong side

☐ Color A: Sand (MC)

▨ Color C: Sage

■ Color B: Nut

hat

Loosely cast on 72 (81) stitches. Join to work in the round, being careful not to twist stitches, place a marker to indicate beginning of round.

Begin stockinette stitch in the round (knit every round); work even for 12 rounds.

Begin working reverse stockinette stitch ridges from Color Ridge Chart; when ridges are complete, continue to work even in stockinette stitch until hat measures 4 (5)"[10 (13)cm] from the base of the rolled edge.

Shape top: Changing to DPN when too few stitches for circular needles
Round 1: * K4, k2tog; repeat from * around to last 0 (3) stitches, end k0 (3)—60 (68) stitches remain.
Round 2: * K3, k2tog; repeat from * around to last 0 (3) stitches, end k0 (3)—48 (55) stitches remain.
Round 3: * K2, k2tog; repeat from * around to last 0 (3) stitches, end k0 (3)—36 (42) stitches remain.
Round 4: * K1, k2tog; repeat from * around—24 (28) stitches remain.
Round 5: K2tog around—12 (14) stitches remain.
Round 6: Knit one round even.
Round 7: Repeat Round 5—6 (7) stitches remain.

finishing

Cut yarn, leaving a 12" (30cm) tail. Thread yarn end through yarn needle and draw through all remaining stitches. Pull tightly and secure tail. Weave in all ends. Allow lower edge to roll up.

elfin bonnet

A garter stitch rectangle is just about one of the simplest things you can knit. With a little color play, a beautiful organic cotton Greenspun yarn, and one easy seam, you get the cutest little bonnet! By simply alternating colors every two rows in garter stitch, you also end up with fun textural stripes. Finish it off with a coordinating ribbon tie, and it's all set for your favorite little elfin child.

SIZES: 6–12 (12–24) MONTHS (SHOWN IN SIZE 12-24 MONTHS)
CIRCUMFERENCE: 16 (18)"[41 (46)CM]

yarn

1 skein of Green Mountain Spinnery Cotton Comfort (80% fine wool, 20% Organic Cotton; 2oz[57g]/ 180yd[166m]) in Bluet (MC) and 1 skein in Mint (CC)

needles

Size 6 (4mm), or size to obtain gauge

notions

Measuring tape
Yarn needle
Scissors
1 yd (1m) of coordinating ribbon; 1¹/₂" (3.8cm) wide
Sewing needle and thread
Straight pins

gauge

20 stitches and 40 rows = 4" (10cm) in garter stitch
Check the gauge before you begin.

bonnet

Loosely cast on 80(90) stitches. With MC, work for 16 rows/8 ridges in garter stitch, ending with a WS row.

Next row (RS): Join CC and begin working in garter stitch stripes as follows, beginning with Rows 3 and 4:

Rows 1 (RS) and 2: With MC, knit.
Rows 3 and 4: With CC, knit.

Continue to work in garter stitch stripes until piece measures 8¹/₂" (21cm), or desired depth from the front of bonnet to the back of head. Loosely bind off all stitches.

Sew back seam: Fold the piece in half and sew together the bind-off edge; the 8-ridge garter stitch band worked at cast-on will frame the face; the back seam forms the base of the bonnet and the elfin point at the top.

Attach ribbon tie: Fold ribbon in half, aligning center of ribbon with the back seam. Pin the ribbon along the inside of the lower edge and, invisibly, but securely, stitch in place, allowing the ribbon extensions to hang free for under-chin tie.

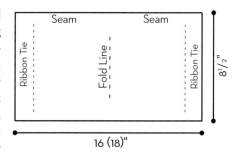

baby bottle cozies

What baby wants to drink from a cold bottle? (Mine certainly won't!) This cute little cozy allows you to keep those bottles warm for the road, for the walk, or for the baby who chooses to snooze in the middle of a feeding. This little snuggly is also a great way to try out new knitting skills. The perfect stash-yarn project, it makes a fabulous, quick-to-knit gift.

FINISHED MEASUREMENTS: TO FIT BOTTLE 7" (18CM) TALL AND 8¾" (22CM) IN CIRCUMFERENCE

NOTES *To adapt the pattern for a taller bottle, simply knit the required number of additional inches.*

Instructions are given for DK-weight yarn first, followed by worsted-weight yarns in parentheses.

yarn

1 skein of MC and small amounts of CCs (DK or worsted weight) for intarsia motifs

Heart Cozy shown in Manos del Uruguay Heavy Worsted Weight (100% wool) in Persimmon (MC) and Brick (CC)

Star Cozy shown in Pachuko (100% color-grown organic cotton) in Vanilla (MC) and Café (CC)

needles

For DK-weight yarn: Size 6 (4mm); size 4 (3.5mm) for ribbing

For worsted-weight yarn: Size 7 (4.5mm); size 5 (3.75mm) for ribbing

notions

Measuring tape

Yarn needle

Scissors

Markers (if desired for intarsia charts)

Cable needle (optional if you are adding a cable)

gauge

DK yarn: 22 stitches and 30 rows = 4" (10cm) in stockinette stitch

Worsted-weight yarn: 20 stitches and 28 rows = 4" (10cm) in stockinette stitch

NOTE *Since different yarns will be used and this is not a garment, gauge is not crucial. Still, it's a good idea to make a swatch to see if you can get close to the suggested gauge, changing the needle size if necessary.*

techniques

Intarsia (see page 138)

TIPS *Knit the cozy plain and simple from a multicolor yarn, or challenge yourself a little—add intarsia motifs, or try out a cable. Heart and star charts are given here for you to experiment with—or pull out your favorite stitch dictionary and jump in.*

If adding a cable to the cozy, place it at the center of the cozy as follows: Subtract the number of stitches in the cable pattern from the total number of stitches. Then, divide that number by 2. The result will be the number of stitches to work before and after the cable pattern.

cozies

With smaller needles and MC, cast on 53 (43) stitches. Work in 1/1 rib for 3" (7.6cm). Change to larger needles and begin working in stockinette stitch; when piece measures 7" (18cm), or desired length, from cast-on edge, end with a WS row.

Shape bottom:

Row 1 (RS): K2, k2tog across, end k1 (3)—41 (36) stitches remain.
Row 2: Purl.
Row 3: K2tog across, end k1 (0)—21 (18) stitches remain.
Row 4: Purl.

Cut yarn, leaving a 12" (30cm) tail. Thread tail through yarn needle, draw yarn through all stitches, pulling them tightly together and securing them. Sew seam.

For intarsia motifs: When piece measures 3½" (9cm) from cast-on edge, join CC.

Begin work from motif chart as follows: On RS, knit across 18 (13) stitches, place a marker (pm), work 17 (17) stitches from chart, pm, knit to end. Work Rows 2-20 from Chart (see below). Cut CC; continue with MC in stockinette stitch as above.

Motif Charts

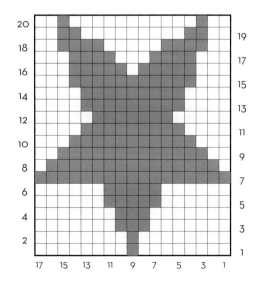
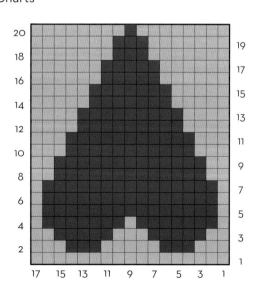

Handwork: The Work of Our Hands, Our Hearts, and the Earth

In our fast-paced world of ever-increasing automation, industrialization, and computerization, a handcrafted item is a special joy. The feel of soft, natural cloth, the beauty of hand-painted yarn, and the love that goes into growing organic fabrics can be healing antidotes to our hurry-up world, where we and our children are surrounded by synthetic materials, plastic toys, and too many pressures.

A handmade item embodies an intention. We instinctively fill it with thoughts and blessings for the person or child for whom it is meant. When we make beautiful things, we engage our whole being and create an expression of our spirit. Handwork establishes a special connection to the tradition of craft and to all the hands that have stitched, knit, sewn, and created before us. Handwork engages us and lets us be focused and calm, realizing that the process is just as important as the product. Furthermore, it represents a lasting piece, a record of our work and of the uniqueness of our youngster's childhood.

The metaphors of handwork give us many opportunities to explore both the natural world and our own personal development. We learn to appreciate the richness and immense value of the materials, our abilities, and how we use our time. We develop patience when reworking something that turned out not quite right, and we learn to accept an "imperfection" as a part of the beauty of a handcrafted piece. We model for our children the love, appreciation, and acceptance of good work, the beauty in simple things, and the importance of supporting and respecting the natural world. As we set an example for a way of living simply yet richly, our children can develop a deep respect for natural materials, the joy of play, and the joy of work.

botanical argyle vest

This classic vest features the rich and beautiful colors of natural plant-dyed and Greenspun yarns. The harmonious colors of the wool-mohair blend yarn are hand-dyed using all-natural plant dyes. This cozy, core-warming piece makes use of the subtle play of like-toned colors by teaming them up with fun-to-knit geometric argyle motifs. The diamonds are knit in intarsia, with crisscross lines added later in duplicate stitch, perfect for newcomers to the technique.

SIZES: TO FIT 12–18 (24) MONTHS (SHOWN IN SIZE 12–18 MONTHS)

CIRCUMFERENCE AT UNDERARM: 26 (28)"[66 (71)CM]

TOTAL LENGTH: 12 (13½)"[30 (34)CM]

yarn

1 skein in Botanical Shades Worsted Singles (60% mohair, 40% wool; 4 oz[114.4g]/225 yd[207m]) in Wasabi (MC) and 1 skein each in Indigo (CC1) and in Cornsilk (CC2), or color combinations of choice

needles

Size 8 (5mm), or size to obtain gauge

Size 7 (4.5mm) 16" (40cm) circular

notions

Scissors

Spare needle (for three-needle bind-off)

Stitch holders

Size J/10 (6mm) crochet hook

Yarn needle

Bobbins (optional for intarsia)

gauge

18 stitches and 22 rows = 4" (10cm) in stockinette stitch

Check the gauge before you begin.

techniques

Duplicate stitch (see page 140), intersia (see page 138), three-needle bind-off (see description on page 139)

back

With MC and smaller needles, loosely cast on 57 (63) stitches. Begin garter stitch; work even for 4 ridges/8 rows, ending with a WS row.

Change to larger needles and stockinette stitch; work even until piece measures 6½ (7½)"[16.5 (19)cm] from cast-on edge, ending with a WS row.

Shape armholes: Bind off 4 (5) stitches at beg of next two rows—49 (53) stitches remain. Decrease 1 stitch each side every other row 4 times—41 (45) stitches remain. Continuing in stockinette stitch, work even until piece measures 11¾ (13¼)"[29 (33)cm] from cast-on edge.

Shape back neck: Work across 10 (12) stitches, bind off center 21 stitches for neck, work to end—10 (12) stitches at each side for shoulders. Working each side separately, work even, if necessary, until piece measures

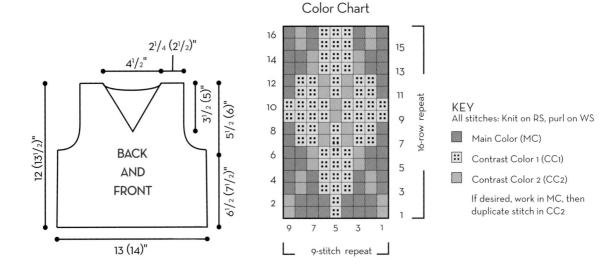

Color Chart

KEY
All stitches: Knit on RS, purl on WS

▨ Main Color (MC)

▣ Contrast Color 1 (CC1)

▨ Contrast Color 2 (CC2)

If desired, work in MC, then
duplicate stitch in CC2

12 (13½)"/30 (34)cm from cast-on edge. Place shoulder stitches on separate
stitch holders.

front

With MC and smaller needles, loosely cast on 57 (63) stitches.

Begin garter stitch; work even for 4 ridges/8 rows, ending with a WS row.

Change to larger needles and stockinette stitch.

Establish pattern: K24 (27) stitches; pm, beginning Row 1 of Color Chart, work
across next 9 stitches from row 1 of chart; K24 (27). Continuing as set, work even
until piece measures 6½ (7½)"[16.5 (19)cm] from cast-on edge, ending with a
WS row.

Shape armholes: Bind off 4 (5) stitches at beg of next two rows—49 (53)
stitches remain. Decrease 1 stitch each side every other row 4 times—41 (45)
stitches remain. AT THE SAME TIME, when piece measures approximately 8½"
(21.5cm) from beginning, end with Row 16 (WS row) of chart. (Three repeats of
chart have been worked.)

Shape front neck: On RS row, work across 20 (22) stitches, bind off center
stitch, add second ball of yarn, work to end—20 (22) stitches at each side for
shoulders.

Working each side separately, using one skein of yarn for each side, work 1 row
even.

A LITTLE BIT ABOUT MOHAIR

Mohair is the fur of the angora, or mohair, goat. The fiber is collected by brushing the animals rather than shearing them, such as is done with sheep. Mohair fiber is very long, and the staple (the length of an animal fiber) is often several inches and has a lovely luster and sheen. Some varieties of mohair are very curly and can be spun to take advantage of this fact. Mohair also has a fuzzy quality and can be spun to be a very fluffy, furry yarn called brushed mohair. Perhaps best of all, mohair is very warm and strong. When combined with wool, it lends a terrific sheen to the finished yarn as well as lots of added warmth. Knitting with mohair that is spun in a traditional way is not much different from knitting with wool, but you will notice its hairy quality as it fluffs a bit when you run your hands through it. Some kinds of 100% mohair yarns can be a bit scratchy and are perfect for making outer and over garments, such as a vest. The gorgeous wool-mohair blend that is featured here in the Botanical Argyle Vest project is spun as a regular single ply yarn and is perfect for keeping the core of those little bodies warm, warm, warm.

Decrease 1 stitch at each side of neck edge this row, then every other row 9 times—10 (12) stitches remain each shoulder.

Work even until total length measures 12 (13½)"[30 (34)cm] from cast-on edge, or same as the back. Place remaining shoulder stitches on separate stitch holders.

Join shoulders: With right sides facing, join shoulders using the three-needle bind-off technique.

finishing

Weave in ends. Sew side seams. Working in duplicate stitch lines on diamonds on the front.

Neckband

With RS facing, circular needle, and CC2, using a crochet hook to assist, beginning at the left shoulder seam, pick up and knit 66 (78) stitches evenly around neck opening as follows: 20 (26) stitches along left front neck shaping, one stitch at center front (base of V-neck), 20 (26) stitches along right front neck shaping edge and 25 stitches across back neck. Place a marker (pm) if desired to mark beginning of round.

Work even in garter stitch in-the-round (knit one round, purl one round) for 4 rounds, shaping band at V-neck as follows:
Rnd 1: K18 (24), k2tog, k1, SSK, knit to end of round.
Rnd 2: Purl.
Rnd 3: K16 (22), k2tog, k1, SSK, knit to end of round.
Rnd 4: Purl.
Bind off all stitches loosely in knit.
Weave in ends.

Armhole bands

With RS facing, circular needle, and CC2, using crochet hook to assist, beginning at underarm seam, pick up and knit 60 (64) stitches evenly around armhole. Pm if desired to mark beginning of round. Work 2 ridges/4 rows in garter stitch in-the-round. Loosely bind off all stitches in knit.

Weave in ends.
Lightly steam block, only if needed.

luxurious nursing shawl

This is a beautiful, simple-to-knit lacy shawl that a nursing mom will find indispensable. Knit in luxurious organic alpaca, this shawl is stunning and easy to wear. It's perfect on a chilly day, for nursing or on its own as a new addition to mom's wardrobe. This shawl allows mom to nurse baby discreetly while keeping them both warm during this special time. The shawl is knit as a large rectangle, then sewn partway on one side to create a poncholike shape.

Wear the shawl pulled over your head poncho fashion for nursing or for covering up on a chilly day. To wear the piece as a scarf, you can either drape it around your neck in double thickness, or, once you've draped it, pull the short end through the neck opening cravat-style. This shawl is great to wear with either a simple jacket or a favorite sweater.

SIZE: 15" (38CM) DEEP BY 72" (1.83M) AROUND (WHEN SEAMED AND WORN)
FINISHED MEASUREMENTS: 15" (38CM) WIDE X 72" (1.83M) LONG

yarn

8 skeins of Blue Sky Alpaca Baby Alpaca (100% Natural Luxury Baby Alpaca; 1¾oz[50g]/ 110yd[100m]) in Medium Gray

needles

Size 8 (5mm), or size to obtain gauge

notions

Measuring tape
Yarn needle
Scissors
Stitch markers (optional)

gauge

16 stitches and 26 rows = 4" (10cm) in stockinette stitch
Check the gauge before you begin.

techniques

Increase (see page 138)

TIPS This pattern features a simple lace-and-cable combination stitch. It is perfect for the knitter who knows how to cable and wants to work on an easy-to-knit project using more than one technique. The lace stitches are created with the use of yarn overs. Yarn over (YO) is a technique for intentionally creating holes in knitting. Making a YO is just as it sounds—you wrap the yarn over the top of the needle. YOs are paired up with decreases, such as a knit two together (k2tog). When you make a YO you are making a new stitch. To compensate for adding a stitch, you decrease in another part of the pattern to keep the number of the stitches on the needle balanced and to make the pretty in and out movement of the lace pattern.

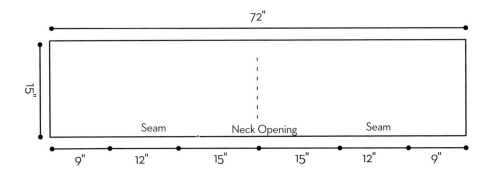

72"

15"

Seam   Neck Opening   Seam

9"   12"   15"   15"   12"   9"

nursing shawl

Cast on 72 stitches. Begin garter stitch; work 8 rows/4 ridges.

Set pattern from chart below as follows: Row 1: K4 (work these 4 stitches in garter stitch throughout as a side border); work the 17-stitch repeat from chart, (Stitches 5–21) three times, placing a marker between repeats, if desired; work Stitches 22–32 from chart once; k4 (work these 4 stitches in garter stitch throughout as a side border).

Continue in the manner as set, repeating Rows 1–8 for pattern, until piece measures approximately 71" (1.8m) or desired length, minus 1" (2.5cm) for garter stitch border, ending with RS Row 7 of the chart.

To complete the shawl, (WS): work 8 rows/4 ridges in garter stitch. Loosely bind off all stitches.

finishing

Block lightly if needed.

top edge seam

Fold shawl in half, bringing the short ends together with right sides facing. Along the long end measure 15" (38cm) from center fold toward short ends. This 15" (38cm) section is the neck opening. Mark this location. Beginning at marker, working along the long side, sew together at garter stitch edge for 12" (30cm), leaving remaining section open down to cast-on/bind-off edges. Weave in ends.

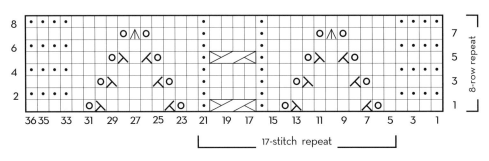

KEY

☐ Knit on right side, purl on wrong side.	⟋ K2tog: Knit 2 stitches together.
⊡ Purl on right side, knit on wrong side.	⟍ Ssk: Slip, slip knit.
⊙ Yarn over	⋀ Double centered dec
	⟋⟍ C4F: Slip 2 stitches to cable needle, hold to front, k2, k2 from cable needle.

ABOUT ALPACA

The Luxurious Nursing Shawl uses a superfine organic alpaca yarn. The alpaca is a longnecked, camel-like animal native to South America. The inner layer of its fur is prized for its loft, extreme softness, and warmth. This fiber, as is true with most luxury fibers, is very short in its staple length and is processed and spun with extra care.

For the yarn to be certified as organic, the alpaca must be treated in the same fashion as animals that produce organic food products, grazing on pesticide-free lands and not being treated with antibiotics or hormones. Certified organic yarn is spun using high-quality food grade organic oils.

The beautiful yarn used for the nursing shawl is the natural color of the animal's down fur. You and your baby will be swaddled in luxury, warmth, and the true essence of nature.

baby bath suite:
chenille robe and washcloth

These pieces are must-haves for bathtub time! Plush organic chenille makes this bathrobe and matching washcloth super thick, soft, and absorbent. An exceptional gift set for a new arrival, this set features bulky, organic color-grown yarn that contributes its own special qualities to the pieces—a velvety fabric (with no chemicals and no dyes) to pamper baby's delicate skin.

chenille robe

SIZE: TO FIT 18–24 MONTHS (TODDLER SIZE 2–4) (SHOWN IN SIZE 2–4)
LENGTH: $16^{1}/_{2}(18^{1}/_{2})$"[42 (47)CM]
SLEEVE LENGTH: 7 (9)"[10 (23)CM], INCLUDING 2" (5CM) CUFF

yarn

3 (4) skeins of Vreseis Ltd Bulky Chenille (100% Foxfibre "colorganic" cotton; 4oz[116g]/150 yd[163m]) in Deep Jade (MC), and

1 skein in Lichen (CC)

NOTE This quantity of yarn should be enough for the entire set.

needles

Size 9 (5.5mm), or size to obtain gauge

Size I/9 (5.5mm) crochet hook for trim

Size US G/6 (4mm) crochet hook for picking up stitches for sleeves (optional)

notions

Measuring tape

Yarn needle

Scissors

Spare needle (for three-needle bind-off)

Stitch holders

gauge

12 stitches and 24 rows = 4" (10cm) in garter stitch

Check the gauge before you begin.

techniques

Three-needle bind-off (see page 139)

robe

NOTE *Because garter stitch looks the same on both sides, placing a marker at the beginning of first RS row makes it easier to work shaping instructions.*

back

With MC, loosely cast on 42 (48) stitches. Begin working in garter stitch; work even until piece measures $11^{1}/_{2}$ (13)"[29 (33)cm] from the cast-on edge, ending with a WS row.

Shape armholes: Bind off 2 stitches at the beginning of the next 2 rows—38 (44) stitches remain.

Work even until piece measures $16^{1}/_{2}$ (18$^{1}/_{2}$)"[42 (47)cm] from the cast-on edge, ending with a WS row.

Shape shoulders and neck: Work 7 (10) stitches; bind off center 24 stitches for neck; work to end—7 (10) stitches remain for each shoulder. Place shoulder stitches on separate holders.

left front

With MC, loosely cast on 21 (24) stitches.

Begin garter stitch; work as for the back, shaping armhole at beginning of RS row, until piece measures 16 (18)"[41 (46)cm] from the cast-on edge, ending with a RS row—19 (22) stitches remain.

Shape neck: (WS) Bind off 12 stitches, work to end— 7 (10) stitches remain for shoulder.

Work even until piece measures same as the back to shoulder. Place remaining stitches on holder.

right front

Work as for the left front, reversing all shapings by shaping armhole at beginning of WS row and neck at beginning of RS row.

Join shoulders: With right sides together, join shoulders using three-needle bind-off method.

sleeve (make 2)

With MC and RS facing, using crochet hook to assist, if desired, pick up and knit 32 (36) stitches around the armhole, beginning and ending at the armhole notches.
Begin working in garter stitch; work even for 2½ (3)"[6.4 (7.6)cm], ending with a WS row.

Shape sleeve: (RS) Decrease 1 stitch each side this row, then every 2½ (3)"[6.4 (7.6)cm] once—28 (32) stitches remain. Work even until sleeve measures 7 (9)"[18 (23)cm] from pick-up row. Bind off all stitches loosely.

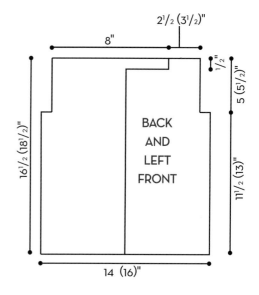

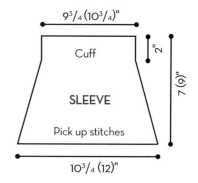

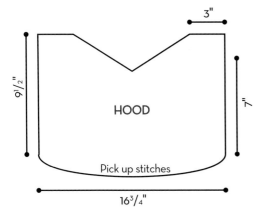

3"

9½"

7"

HOOD

Pick up stitches

16¾"

hood

With MC and RS facing, using crochet hook to assist, if desired, pick up and knit 50 stitches around the neck edge—13 stitches along each front neck, and 24 stitches across the back neck, beginning and ending at the center front.

Begin garter stitch; work even for 6 (7)"[15 (18)cm] from the pick-up row, ending with a WS row; place a marker between 2 center stitches.

Shape hood: Work across to marker; join a second ball of yarn and work to end. Working each side separately, decrease 1 stitch each side of center every row 15 times—10 stitches remain each side.

Work even until piece measures 8½ (9½)"[21.6 (24)cm] from the pick-up row. Bind off remaining stitches. Sew center seam.

belt

With CC, loosely cast on 6 stitches.

Begin garter stitch; work even until piece measures 48" (122cm), or desired length. Bind off all stitches.

finishing

Sew sleeve and side seams.

Weave in all ends.

edging

With RS facing, using crochet hook and CC, join yarn with a slip stitch to the lower right front corner of robe; ch 1, work 1 row of single crochet evenly up the right front, around the hood opening, and down the left front to the lower left front corner. Fasten off. Weave in ends.

Attach the belt to center of the back at the waist.

chenille wash cloth

FINISHED MEASUREMENTS: APPROXIMATELY 6" (15CM) SQUARE

yarn

1 skein of Vreseis Ltd Bulky
    Chenille (4oz/116g; 150 yd/163m;
    100% Foxfibre "colorganic"
    cotton) in Lichen

NOTE *Left-over yarn from robe
should be enough to knit
washcloth.*

needles

Size 9 (5.5 mm), or size to obtain
    gauge

notions

Measuring tape
Yarn needle
Scissors

gauge

12 stitches and 24 rows = 4" (10cm)
    in garter stitch
Check the gauge before you begin.

washcloth

Loosely cast on 18 stitches.

Begin working in garter stitch; work even until piece measures 6"
(15cm) from the cast-on edge or until square. Bind off all stitches
loosely.

Infant Massage:
The Power of Loving Touch

The power of loving touch is extraordinary. Touch can communicate, heal, relieve stress, and even transfer a blessing or positive energy from one person to another. One of the most effective and available forms of healing with touch is massage.

Baby massage offers a precious and powerful opportunity for bonding and relationship building, and the benefits are manifold. Studies show that premature or ill babies who regularly receive gentle massage gain weight faster and are more likely to thrive. Infant massage has also been shown to aid digestion, boost the immune system, improve circulation, and make baby feel loved and cared for. The elements of infant massage can sooth, assist healing, calm a frightened or fussy child, or simply become an enjoyable part of the bath-time ritual. Infant massage is also a magnificent and mutually rewarding way for parents and baby to bond and begin early forms of communication.

Your basic instincts can guide you in your choice of how to massage baby and when. Your baby will give you cues as to whether he or she is enjoying the experience, or if you should try another time. Use your instincts as your guide as you lovingly caress your baby's legs, toes and face. Following are some extremely basic tips for using gentle massage on your baby. To begin, make certain you have a comfortable, warm place to massage your baby. Consider having a warm blanket on hand to maintain a cozy temperature. It is extremely important to keep the environment warm so as to prevent baby from loosing body heat. Also, wear clothing you won't mind spattering with a bit of massage oil. After bath time is often a great choice, when baby is relaxed and his or her skin is warm. If your baby seems bothered by the massage, try again at another time.

For further information about infant massage, or to locate a qualified trainer to teach you more about the benefits and techniques of infant massage, please visit the International Association of Infant Massage (IAIM) online at www.iaim.net or www.infantmassageusa.org.

projects from felt

Besides knitting with natural and organic fibers, another way we can be good to the environment through our handwork is by recycling old sweaters and using them as felt. Felt can be made from sweaters or pieces of knitting by subjecting them to hot water and friction (see page 62 for more detailed instructions). This shrinks the fibers and makes a dense, solid fabric. The resulting felt takes on varying degrees of thickness, allowing you to make a clean cut edge and alter it easily.

Making recycled felt is one big, fun experiment, but creating it from old sweaters is very, very easy. First, you will need to collect old sweaters, which can be found in secondhand shops (and perhaps even in your own closet). In order to make felt, the fiber content must be composed of all-or nearly all-natural animal fibers or blends of natural fibers. Look for contents such as pure wool, lambs wool, mohair, cashmere, angora, and camel. If you find a sweater with more than 80 percent natural animal fiber, give it a try. Baby will love the wonderful, soft clothing and toys you create from recycled felt and you will love how easy they are to sew.

Making Recycled Felt

Making recycled felt is one big experiment. There is really no way to know just how a sweater will felt—how thick it will be, how fuzzy it will be, how fast or slow it will shrink. With a little patience and experience, you'll get a sense of what works best. Some fibers will felt very thick and hard, while others, like lamb's wool, will felt very soft, fuzzy, and pliable.

Recycled felt is made from fabric knit from all-natural animal fibers such as wool, lambs wool, angora, or cashmere. Start by sorting your raw material (that is, old sweaters and knitted swatches) into like colors. The felting process creates a lot of fluff and lint; one way to keep things under control is to place the sweaters in zippered pillowcases or net lingerie bags. When I am making recycled felt, I actually stop and strain out the blobs of fluff from the top of the water every once in a while.

Place the sweaters in your washing machine, and fill it with hot water (colder temperatures will not work) and a very small amount of detergent. Dish soap works very well. The felting process works best with a top-loading machine as you might need to open the lid periodically to check the progress and strain the lint. Start a regular wash cycle. Check the progress of your felt once or twice during the wash cycle. You should be able to feel the difference in the fabric as it felts—it will become firmer and denser. If you don't feel any changes taking place, turn the dial back and allow the wash cycle to run again. Once you are satisfied, allow a cold rinse and spin cycle to do their thing.

Lay your newly made felt out flat to dry. During warmer weather, I place my recycled felt out on a metal mesh patio table. Do be aware that your felt will dry in whatever shape you lay it in. Some of the inevitable warps and curves can be blocked out later with steam.

You might try experimenting with running your pieces through the drier to see what happens. It may make things firmer, or softer, or it may do nothing but make them misshapen. Again, it's an experiment every time you do it—so remember to keep your sense of adventure. Once your felted pieces are dry, they are ready to cut.

recycled wool toddler jacket

This little jacket is cut right from the shape of a shrunken sweater—no seams to sew! Start by felting a bunch of sweaters. Choose the one that is the size you want, and cut out a neckline, cut down the center front, and cut the sleeves to the right length. Then add the trim of your choice—embroidered blanket stitch, single crochet, or something you sew on. Cut buttonholes if desired, or knit on cuffs and a front band. Take it a step further by adding a felt appliqué, like the little truck shown here. The jacket shown was made from an adult hooded sweater.

SIZE TO FIT APPROXIMATELY 18–24 MONTHS
(SIZE WILL DEPEND ON THE SWEATER AND THE RATE AT WHICH IT FELTS)

materials

Natural fiber sweaters felted in
    washing machine (see page 62)
Scraps of felt for appliqué
    (optional)

notions

Sharp fabric scissors
Ruler
Chalk
Embroidery needle and floss
Sewing needle and thread
Braided trim or ribbon (optional)
Buttons
Toggles or frogs for closures
    (optional)

sewing techniques

Embroidery stitches: Blanket stitch
(see page 140), whipstitch (see
page 141)

TIPS *Use a blanket stitch or whipstitch in bright contrasting colors of floss or yarn to create a decorative edging for this little jacket and help reinforce the cut edges of felt and keep them from curling.*

starting out

Select a batch of sweaters based on their fiber content, design elements, and size. I have found that prefelted sweaters, sized women's medium to men's small, generally felt to the perfect size to fit a one- to two-year-old. Remember, felted size varies widely, so there is an element of experimentation to this project—which adds to the fun! Consider using sweaters that contain lamb's wool, angora, or cashmere to create the softest finished jackets.

making the jacket

After felting a batch of sweaters, allow them to dry and evaluate them for size and fit, or comparing them to one of your child's garments that fits well.

Once you have selected the sweater, using your ruler and chalk, draw a straight line up the center front of the piece. With sharp fabric scissors, cut along this line. That's it! Decorate and embellish as desired (truck motif template is shown here, or consider using appliqué templates from other projects in this book). Finish edges with whipstitch or blanket stitch (also called buttonhole stitch), or sew on purchased or trim or ribbon. Cut buttonholes if desired and sew buttons securely opposite the buttonholes. Other ideas for closures are frogs, clasps, or toggles.

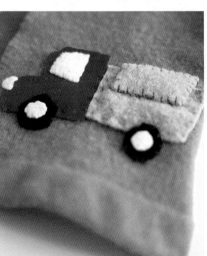

quartet of hats

These crazy, fun, and funky hats can be made in limitless combinations of style and embellishment. As you complete each beautiful, one-of-kind creation, please make sure your threads are knotted and tied off securely, so that the embellishments are not easily picked off by curious fingers.

crazy crown hat

SIZE: TO FIT 9–18 (24–36) MONTHS (SHOWN IN SIZE 9–18 MONTHS)
CIRCUMFERENCE: APPROXIMATELY 18 (20) [46 (51)CM]

materials

2 pieces of recycled felt,
    approximately 9" x 7" (23x18cm)
Scrap felt for embellishment

notions

Paper for making patterns
Scissors
Sewing needle and thread
Sewing machine (optional, may be
    stitched entirely by hand)
Embroidery needle and
    embroidery floss
Straight pins
Chalk

sewing techniques

Hand embroidery stitches:
Whipstitch (see page 141), blanket
stitch (see page 140), chain stitch
(see page 140), simple running
stitch (see page 141)

TEMPLATE PAGE 133

making the hat

Create a pattern from the rectangular hat template. Cut two pieces of felt from pattern; these may be two of the same color, or two different colors.

Cut out three pieces from the crown edge template in colors of your choice. Two different colors are used in the hat shown—the two pieces at the lower edge are of one color and the third at the top of the hat is in another.

Using chalk, randomly draw three or four swirls on the rectangle pieces. Using embroidery floss in the colors of your choice and chain stitch, follow chalk lines to sew spirals.

Next, select the seaming style you wish to use for your hat—whipstitch, running stitch, or blanket stitch. With wrong sides together, sew both side seams in style you have selected, leaving top and bottom open. Insert Top crown piece. In running stitch using embroidery thread, sew across top through all three thicknesses. If your top crown needs a little bit of stability, consider sewing a running stitch in coordinating embroidery floss up and down the points (see photo).

Next, apply the lower edge crown trim to bottom opening of hat. Pin one piece of crown edging to front and one to back, making sure head opening is still open. With embroidery floss and color of your choice stitch all the way around lower circumference of hat. Then, with needle and thread, sew the sides of the crown edging together on both sides of hat.

circles-and-squares hat

SIZE: TO FIT 9–18 (24–36) MONTHS (SHOWN IN SIZE 9–18 MONTHS)
CIRCUMFERENCE: APPROXIMATELY 18 (20)"[46 (51CM)]

materials

2 pieces of recycled felt,
   approximately 9" x 7" (23x18cm)
Scrap felt for embellishment

notions

Paper for making patterns
Scissors
Sewing needle and thread
Sewing machine (optional, may be
   stitched entirely by hand)
Straight pins
Embroidery needle and
   embroidery floss

sewing techniques

Hand embroidery stitches:
Whipstitch (see page 141), blanket
stitch (see page 140), chain stitch
(see page 140), simple running
stitch (see page 141)

TEMPLATE PAGE 130

making the hat

Create a pattern from the rectangular hat template. Cut two pieces of felt from pattern; these may be two of the same color, or two different colors.

Cut out circles in various sizes and colors. Using embroidery floss in your choice of color, sew the circles to the rectangular felt pieces using a running stitch. Lay the circles out in a random pattern, overlapping some if you like.

Next, select the seaming style you wish to use for your hat. You will be seaming the sides and top of the hat. If you wish the seams to be on the inside (as shown), use sewing thread in a coordinating color and place pieces with right sides facing (sewing machine may also be used if you wish). Beginning at one of the lower side edges, sew tightly with a running stitch up the side, across the top, and down the other side. Turn right-side out and steam lightly if desired.

decorating the hat

For a more decorative look, you may choose to use embroidery floss and a running stitch or whipstitch on the outside of your hat. To do this, place pieces with wrong sides together. Using floss in the color of your choice and an embroidery needle, begin at lower edge, sew up the side, across the top, and down the other side.

To make tassels, cut two rectangles from scrap felt approximately 2" by 4" (5x10cm). With sharp scissors, cut down the rectangles part way (the long way) into fourths. Cut down about 3" (7.6cm) and leave 1" (2.5cm) intact so you still have one piece of felt with four fringes. Fold the piece in half, matching long sides, and using sewing thread and needle, invisibly hand stitch to the top corners of the hat. Repeat for other side.

top knot hat

SIZE: TO FIT 9–18 (24–36) MONTHS (SHOWN IN SIZE 9–18 MONTHS)
CIRCUMFERENCE: APPROXIMATELY 18 (20)"[46 (51)CM]

materials

*2 pieces of recycled felt,
    approximately 9" x 7" (23x8cm),
    in two different colors*
*Additional pieces large enough to
    cut 2 rectangles approximately
    10" x 4" (25x10cm)*

notions

Paper for making patterns
Scissors
Sewing needle and thread
*Sewing machine (optional, may be
    stitched entirely by hand)*
Straight pins

sewing techniques

*Hand or machine sewing using
simple running stitch (see page 141)*

TEMPLATE PAGES 131-132

making the hat

Create a pattern from the top knot hat template. Cut two pieces of felt from pattern; these may be two of the same color, or two different colors. (Hat shown uses two different colors.)

sewing the hat

With right sides together, sew both side seams by machine or by hand using tight running stitch, leaving top open. Trim seams close to stitching, turn right side out, and steam seams flat.

decorating the hat

Cut two pieces from the wave edge template in the felt color of your choice. Sew the two pieces together at the sides with running stitch or by machine. Trim close to the seam. Turn right-side out and steam flat. With hat right side out, pin trim to INSIDE matching seams and straight edges with seams of trim showing. Stitch with tight running stitch or by machine and trim close to stitching. Turn trim back to the outside so the RS of trim is showing and the WS is up against the outside of hat, and steam seams, flattening trim against hat.

lazy daisy hat

SIZE: TO FIT 9-18 (24-36) MONTHS (SHOWN IN SIZE 9-18 MONTHS)
CIRCUMFERENCE APPROXIMATELY 18 (20)"[45.72 (50.8)CM]

materials

2 pieces of recycled felt,
approximately 9" x 7" (23x8cm)
Scrap felt for embellishment

notions

Paper for making patterns
Scissors
Sewing needle and thread
Sewing machine (optional, may
be stitched entirely by hand)
Straight pins
Embroidery needle and
embroidery floss

sewing techniques

Hand embroidery stitches:
Hand or machine sewing using
simple running stitch (see page 141)

TEMPLATE PAGES 132-133

making the hat

Create a pattern from the rounded top template. Cut two pieces of felt from pattern.

This hat uses a simple flower shape and leaves for embellishment and a triangle pointed trim at the bottom edge. You can also play around with all of these hats by choosing to embellish them with designs from the templates for the Play Blox (see page 119) and let your imagination be your guide.

making the daisies

Copy the template, cut the desired number of flowers, flower centers, and leaves from your chosen colors of felt. Here, classic daisy colors are used. Stitch the flowers onto the hat where they look best using coordinating sewing threads and simple running stitch. Then add the circles in the center of each flower, and one or two leaves to each flower.

sewing the hat

To seam the hat, put RS facing each other and sew tightly with a running stitch, or use a sewing machine. Beginning at one of the lower side edges, sew tightly with a running stitch up the side, around the top, and down the other side. Turn right-side out and steam lightly if desired.

Lower edge trim

Cut two pieces from the crown edge template in felt color of your choice. Sew the two pieces together at the sides with running stitch or by machine. Trim close to seam. Turn right-side out and steam flat. Pin trim to INSIDE, matching seams and straight edges with seams of trim showing. Stitch with tight running stitch or by machine, and trim close to stitching. Turn trim back to the outside so right side of trim is showing and WS is up against the outside of hat, and steam seams, flattening trim against hat.

hot-water bottle cover

A hot-water bottle can become a new best friend to either an expecting or a new mom. There is nothing like the gentle, moist, soothing heat a hot-water bottle provides to relieve aches and give simple comfort. A soft felt cover can be as simple or as ornate as desired. Use a subtle pattern or the pattern of a recycled wool sweater alone, or embellish a flat recycled or handmade wool surface with some cut felt shapes or an embroidered monogram. Not for mom's exclusive use, bottles filled with warm water can warm up the bassinet before laying baby down for a cozy sleep on a chilly night.

FINISHED MEASUREMENTS: TO FIT STANDARD HOT-WATER BOTTLE, APPROXIMATELY 8" (20CM) WIDE BY 14" (36CM) TALL.

materials

*2 pieces of recycled felt,
    approximately 9" x 15" (23x38cm)*
Scrap felt for embellishment
*Embroidery needle and
    embroidery floss*

notions

Paper for making patterns
Scissors
Sewing needle and thread

sewing techniques

*Embroidery stitches: Whipstitch
(see page 141), buttonhole stitch
(see page 140), simple running
stitch (see page 141)*

TEMPLATE PAGES 119, 127

making the hot-water bottle cover

Copy the pattern for the hot-water bottle cover onto paper. Using this paper pattern, cut two identical pieces from recycled felt. The pattern shows options for either a straight top or a wavy top. Cut as you choose.

decorating the hot-water bottle cover

The covers shown feature two different appliqués. Apply decorative motifs to the outsides of your hot water bottle cover pieces before assembly. Of the covers shown, the green cover features the flower appliqué from the "Lazy Daisy Hat" and the white cover features a single red heart.

For the daisy motif, decide how many flowers you would like to feature on your hot water bottle cover, and follow the instructions for making daises (page 72). For the heart appliqué, cut out a heart from desired colored felt using the heart template. Using desired color embroidery floss and embroidery needle, sew the heart onto the outside of the front piece of felt for the body of the cover using buttonhole or whip stitch.

Think about experimenting with different colors of felt and different motifs. Consider using appliqués and decorative elements from the "Play Blox" (see page 119) or the other templates in the book to make each cover unique and playful.

With wrong sides together, sew the two pieces together, leaving the top of the cover open. Use the embroidery stitch of your choice (blanket/buttonhole, whipstitch, or running stitch). The heart cover features blanket/buttonhole stitch. For added decoration, the bottle features a thin band of felt to match the heart around the opening. If you choose to include this decorative element, you could also consider using a coordinating ribbon. If you are planning to use this cover for a baby, be sure all decorative elements are sewn on securely.

inserting the hot-water bottle

Once your cover is complete, gently fold an empty hot-water bottle in half and slide it into the top opening, allowing it to unfold and lie flat once inside the cover. Please note: The hot-water bottles can make surfaces very hot, so if you are using your bottle directly on skin, or to warm a baby's bed, use just warm, NOT hot, water.

caring for the hot-water bottle cover

Gently wash your bottle cover as follows when it needs it. Using a no-rinse wool wash, allow the bottle cover to soak in a sink or basin tub filled with warm water. Gently squeeze out excess water. Then run the cover through the spin cycle of your washing machine and allow it to air dry. If you are washing more than one felted item, make sure they are of like colors.

Recycling: Not Just About Paper

We're all familiar with the phrase "reduce, reuse, recycle." But this simple idea extends beyond putting our newspapers out for recycling pick-up and bringing our own bags to the market (both really good ideas!). That middle word—reuse—can apply to so much in our lives. It is true that even the smallest change in the way you live can impact the environment. Being green and living lightly mean using less, consuming wisely, and reusing when we can. We can make these philosophies into realities by finding new and creative uses for old items.

By choosing to reuse, we reduce our personal impact on the planet, reducing the demand for more raw materials as well as reducing the amount of energy, pollutants, and chemicals involved in making something. Buying second-hand items reuses materials, keeping them out of the waste stream and eliminating the need for more goods to be made. By purchasing second-hand within your own town, you lessen the waste stream and keep your money within your local economy.

Reusing breaks the consumerism cycle. Give your baby the preciousness of a handcrafted item while encouraging him or her to believe in a nondisposable society. By walking the walk, you model a low-impact lifestyle while providing your child and friends with enriching, colorful, tactile, natural toys to support their development, to improve their world, and to just plain have fun.

stitched moon and star toys

Have you ever wanted to give your baby the moon and stars? Well, now you can, and the sky is the limit as to how many and how magical you can make them. These tactile, all-natural playthings can be used to snuggle and stimulate baby's sense of touch and developing color perception.

FINISHED MEASUREMENTS: APPROXIMATELY 6" X 6" (15.25 X 15.25CM) FOR MOON AND STAR

materials

Recycled felt: 2 pieces for moon approximately 6½" x 13" (16.5x33cm), 2 pieces for star approximately 7" x 14" (18x36cm)

Wool roving or clean fleece for stuffing

Sturdy yarn or embroidery floss in color(s) of your choice

(Shown: Wool yarn in contrasting shades for outside edges, blue for eyes, red for mouth)

notions

Paper for making patterns
Scissors
Sharp yarn needle
Needle and matching sewing thread

sewing techniques

Embroidery stitches: Blanket stitch (see page 140), whipstitch (see page 141), satin stitch (see page 141)

TEMPLATE PAGE 118

TIPS *Sturdy blanket stitch or whipstitch holds the toys together at the edges, while satin stitch and backstitches are used to create whimsical faces. Satin stitch is used for the eyes and cheeks and back stitches for the mouth.*

starting out

Make the pattern by tracing the moon and star templates onto paper and cutting out the pattern pieces. Using the patterns, cut out two pieces of recycled felt for each moon and each star.

Embroider a simple face, as shown, using satin stitch for the eyes and back stitches for the mouth, in colors of your choice.

making the moon and star toys

The seams may be worked with buttonhole stitch or whipstitch as you choose.

With RS facing outward (WS held together), using yarn needle and yarn or embroidery floss and the embroidery stitch of your choice, stitch around the outside edge of the pieces, making sure that you are stitching through both thicknesses of fabric. Leave an opening 1–2" (2.5–5cm) long to insert the wool filling.

Fill the toys with wool to desired level of fullness. Using yarn or floss and yarn needle, finish stitching around the outside edge, stitching the opening closed.

snuggly felt snake

This s-s-sassy s-s-snake is cut from a single piece of recycled felt—the easiest way is to make him out of the sleeve of a felted sweater. Add little felt pieces for the eyes and tongue, and you have a s-s-smashing all-natural toy. Filled with wool roving, this toy can grow with young babies.

Have fun using the designs of recycled sweaters to decorate your snake. Here, our snake is striped from the grey and red stripes of the original sweater. You might also cut out your pattern piece so that the diamonds of an argyle run down his back. Depending on how you use the sweater designs and embellish with scrap pieces, each critter will be absolutely unique.

FINISHED MEASUREMENTS: APPROXIMATELY 18–24" (46–61CM) LONG

materials
1 piece of recycled felt:
   Approximately 8" (20cm)
   wide x 18–24" (46–61cm) long
Scrap felt for embellishment
   (white for eyes, red for tongue)
Wool roving or fleece for stuffing
Embroidery needle and
   embroidery floss

notions
Paper for making patterns
Scissors
Sewing needle and thread in color
   to coordinate with felt

sewing techniques
Hand embroidery stitches: simple
running stitch (see page 141)

TEMPLATE PAGE 120

making the snake
Copy pattern for snake onto paper. Using this paper pattern, cut one piece on the fold from recycled felt, as shown on the pattern piece.

With right sides together, fold along fold lines with side edges together, and stitch the belly seam closed. Sew the end of the snake closed; turn right-side out. Stuff with wool roving or fleece until the snake is of the desired firmness.

decorating the snake
Cut small circles from felt for eyes, and stitch into place as shown. Sew sides of head closed. Sew tongue in place, and sew mouth shut. If making this project for a very young baby, do sew all pieces on securely.

Keep making snakes, and have each one be different—add scraps of different colors or shapes. Play around with different color eyes. Enjoy!

soft play blox

These adorable play blox are made from embellished felt squares fitted onto foam cubes. Crafted from recycled felt made from old sweaters, they are easy for little hands to manipulate and they provide exciting textures, colors, and tactile sensations to stimulate baby's developing senses. The blox can safely be thrown around or pounded on. Just be sure to sew the appliqué squares on tightly. Simple to wash when needed, the blox are a fun way to develop your design and appliqué skills. Consider making up your own motifs to reflect themes in your baby's environment. You can explore using other types of felt for the appliqué, too—felt scraps remaining from other projects, handmade felt, or purchased wool felt. Let your creativity soar.

FINISHED MEASUREMENTS: EACH BLOCK WILL MEASURE 4" (10CM) SQUARE

materials

Recycled felt in an assortment of bright colors, cut into 4¹/₂ x 4¹/₂" (11x11cm) squares (see more about making recycled felt on page 62)

NOTE *Each block requires 6 squares (a set of 6 blocks requires 36 squares).*

Additional felt pieces/scraps for appliqué
Six 4" (10.2cm) foam cubes

NOTE *For all-natural blox, substitute 1 pound wool roving for foam cubes (the wool will need to be packed tightly for the blox to keep their shape).*

Yarns and embroidery floss in colors of your choice

notions

Sharp-end tapestry needle
Embroidery needle(s)
Sharp scissors
Straight pins
Cardboard for template
Chalk for marking squares from cardboard template

sewing techniques

Embroidery stitches: Blanket/ buttonhole (see page 140), whipstitch (see page 141), french knot (see page 141), simple running stitch (see page 141)

TEMPLATE PAGE 119

starting out

Cut a 4¹/₂" (11cm) square template from cardboard. This will allow a ¹/₄" (6.35mm) selvedge for sewing around the entire edge of the squares. Lay the template on the recycled felt and mark around it with chalk. Cut the squares using sharp scissors. Choose a variety of colors and textures to make things really fun. You can modify the number of squares needed, based on the number of blox you wish to make. For example, if you only wish to make four blox, and each block requires six felt squares, you will need twenty-four squares.

Select your appliqué motifs from the templates given or make up your own simple designs based on a theme for your nursery, a story, or items that are part of your daily life. They must be made in simple and fairly large shapes to fit within an

approximately 3½" (8.9cm) square. Use the same motifs over and over if you like, or make each unique.

Choose two appliqués for each block; for the set of six blocks, you will be making twelve appliqué squares. Select which color squares you will use for the appliqué pieces. Cut out the needed appliqué shapes in the colors of your choice from your additional felt and felt scraps.

making the play blox

Using embroidery floss and embroidery needle, or strong wool yarn threaded through a tapestry needle, sew your appliqués to the chosen squares. Use the blocks shown as suggestions for placement and colors. You can use a whip-stitch, a running stitch, a buttonhole stitch, or invisible stitching to apply your designs. Be sure to sew all pieces on securely, especially small ones, to protect them from curious, prying little fingers. Play around with each to see how they look. They will be cute no matter what! Treat this project as a learning tool and experiment.

assembling

Once the appliqué squares are completed, begin to assemble the blocks as follows:

As shown in the illustration below, using a sharp tapestry needle, strong wool yarn in a color of your choice, and either whip stitch or blanket stitch, sew side 1B to side 2A.

Next, sew side 2B to side 3A as above.

Then, sew side 3B to side 4A.

Finally, bring the sewn piece into a circular shape, and sew side 4B to side 1A. You will now have the exterior of a block.

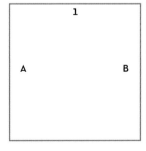 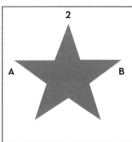 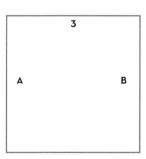 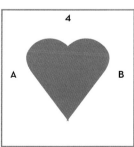

Take one of the remaining unembellished squares and put it in place at the top of the square you have created, as if you were placing a lid on a box. Pin the top into place. Sew around the entire edge of the square, sewing it into place with the wool yarn and the same stitch you have used on the sides. Secure the yarn well and bring your loose end to the inside of the box you have made. If necessary, use a blunt-tipped object (such as a chopstick) to make sure your corners are nice and sharp on the outside.

stuffing

Place the felt blox form over the foam cube, as if you were putting on a sock. It may be necessary to use a blunt-tipped object to help push the corners of the foam cube into the corners of the felt cover. If you are having difficulty, consider turning your felt cover inside out, and folding it over the foam cube, as if you were dressing it. If you choose to use wool or wool roving to fill your blox, stuff the open-sided cube with enough wool to achieve desired firmness.

Place the remaining felt square on the open end of the cube where the foam is exposed. Pin it into place. Stitch it just as for opposite end, securing the yarn end when you are finished and drawing the yarn tail to the inside of the cube.

Repeat these steps for each of the blox. Enjoy watching your baby play with them, discovering their texture and feeling. You may find yourself enjoying them just as much!

lavender-scented bear

Filled with dried lavender flowers and flax seed, this all-natural bean-bag-like toy bear makes a lovely sachet for a little baby's room, but it's also perfect for mom and older babies to play with and toss around. The little bear emits the soothing scent of lavender, and can be refreshed with a couple of drops of essential oil from time to time.

FINISHED MEASUREMENTS: 6¹/₂" (165 CM) TALL

materials

Recycled felt: 2 pieces approximately 7" x 7" (18x18cm)

¹/₄ cup whole flax seed and ¹/₂ cup dried lavender flowers (available at natural food stores), mixed

Essential oil of lavender (optional)

Sturdy yarn or embroidery floss in color(s) of your choice

(Shown: A silk-blend yarn, in a coordinating shade)

notions

Paper for making patterns

Scissors

Sharp yarn needle

Straight pins

Matching sewing thread and needle

sewing techniques

Hand embroidery stitches: Whipstitch (see page 141), blanket stitch (see page 140), chain stitch (see page 140), simple running stitch (see page 141), French knot (see page 141), backstitch (see page 140), satin stitch (see page 141)

TEMPLATE PAGE 121

SEWING TIPS *This bear stuffing is made from scented flax seed, which is quite tiny, so it is best to machine- or hand-stitch around the bear first to help prevent leaks. Leave a small opening for inserting the filling. Then work a decorative hand stitch such as a whipstitch or a blanket/buttonhole stitch with yarn or floss around the edges. The bear shown features a blanket stitch finish.*

starting out

Make a pattern by tracing the bear template onto paper, and cutting out the pattern piece. Cut out two pieces of recycled felt using the pattern for the body.

Embroider a simple face, as shown, using French knots for the eyes and a few back stitches for the mouth. A small patch of satin stitch defines the ears. For a more pronounced face, use black or brown for the eyes and red for the mouth for a more pronounced face.

making the bear

With RS facing outward (WS held together), sew running stitch by hand or machine as previously described. Then, using yarn needle and chosen yarn or thread and the embroidery stitch of your choice, stitch around the outside edge, making sure that you are stitching through both thicknesses of fabric. (Leave an opening 1–2" (2.5–5cm) long between the legs to insert the filling.)

Mix together the flax seed and dried lavender flowers, adding two to three drops of essential oil of lavender if a stronger scent is desired. Fill the bear with the lavender mixture to desired level of fullness. Stitch the opening shut securely. Using yarn or floss and yarn needle, finish stitching around the outside edge, stitching the opening closed.

Aromatherapy: Essential Scents

Aromatherapy is the art of using naturally extracted aromatic essences from botanical sources to balance, harmonize, and promote the health of mind, body, and spirit. Aromatherapy can enhance the body's natural ability to balance, regulate, heal, and maintain itself. Through the use of scent and touch, aromatherapy can enrich and improve mental and physical states of being.

The highly concentrated extracts from plants, herbs, and flowers used in aromatherapy are in the form of essential oils. These oils stimulate the body through skin absorption and inhalation. Essential oils are complex, highly fragrant, and fragile substances containing the most potent and concentrated extracts from various parts of flowers, fruits, leaves, spices, roots, and woods.

In an essential oil, the botanical essence molecules are approximately seventy-five to a hundred times more concentrated than they would be in dried plant form. The most common method of extracting these fragile oils from their source material is through steam distillation, while a cold-expression process is used for citrus oils. Essential oils are intended for external use only.

How do you know if an essential oil is really essential? The label should state that the oil is 100-percent derived from the given botanical source, either by steam distillation or by cold pressing. It should also state that the product is a pure essential oil, not to be confused with a blended, or diluted, product intended for massaging or skin moisturizing. You can purchase essential oils from an aromatherapy practitioner or from most natural product stores. If you are not sure about the purity or appropriateness of an oil, consult a trusted source or an aromatherapy practitioner.

Essential oils affect our bodies in several ways. Their molecular components enter nasal passages where they stimulate the olfactory nerve and send messages directly to the brain. In the brain, they trigger changes in the limbic system, which in turn can stimulate physiological responses within the body via the nervous, endocrine, or immune systems.

Essential oils are delivered in many different ways. Common methods are with diffusers, inhalation, compresses, massage, and in the bath. A diffuser is a device that distributes the scent of an essential oil throughout an indoor environment. In inhalation, a concentrated form of the oil is held closely to the nose. This method allows scent to reach olfactory receptors directly and is best left in the hands of a qualified aromatherapist. A compress treated with essential oil can be applied to specific areas of the body to deliver benefit to a specific region or to treat an anatomically specific ailment. In massage, the essential oil is heavily diluted in a carrier oil—a pure, high-quality oil that is absorbed directly into the skin. And lastly, the bath allows essential oils to be inhaled through steam vapors and to come into direct contact with the skin, where absorption may occur. As with massage, only a few drops are used for an entire tub full of water.

Aromatherapy can address many of the conditions of pregnancy and can be of great benefit to babies. Perhaps the most renowned benefit of aromatherapy to moms and babies is the calming relaxation it helps bring. Just a few of mom's conditions for which aromatherapy can be helpful include fatigue, edema, insomnia, nausea, labor, and nursing. For baby, aromatherapy can address many issues, including colic, fussiness, diaper rash, and teething.

Although aromatherapy is considered a holistic health modality and essential oils are natural substances, the oils are *extremely potent*. Care and education *must* be used when employing aromatherapy techniques during pregnancy or on a baby. The pregnant and newborn bodies are both very delicate, and they react differently to essential extracts. Before using aromatherapy techniques during pregnancy or on your baby, please consult a qualified specialist or reputable reference source. It is important to make certain you are applying the oils safely and that the scents and oils used will have no ill effects on any physical systems or on delicate skin.

For more information on aromatherapy and recommended aromatherapy schools, or how to find a certified aromatherapist in your area, visit the National Association of Holistic Aromatherapy online at www.naha.org.

projects to sew

Nature Babies sewn projects are made from wonderful organic and natural fiber materials, which range from organic flannel and supersoft, color-grown cotton fleece to felt and organic cotton batting. Several handwork techniques and skills are also explored, including machine and hand sewing as well as embroidery and embellishment. Babies will delight in the simple styling and tactile elements of sweet baby dolls and star babies. They will be coddled in softness in an all-organic fleece outfit. Their developing senses and imaginations will be inspired by charming, magical beings. These items, for your own baby or for gift giving, encourage imaginative play, stimulate development, and present baby with natural materials to foster a growing appreciation of our natural world.

As you make these toys, please keep in mind that small parts can come off and babies should never be left alone with anything (or anything whose parts) are small enough to fit in their mouths. Moms should supervise use of these toys with their babies or use them to decorate their babies' rooms.

simple organic baby doll

A classic handwork doll, this project is great for all skill levels—even someone who has never sewn! A basic running stitch helps coax the fabric into shape. The doll's hands and legs are created with simple overhand knots. The simple shape, all-natural and soft organic materials, and minimal detail introduce a baby to tactile sensations and a suggested representation of the human form. Its size makes it easy for little hands to grasp. These dolls are so cute and so cuddly that you'll find yourself making bunches of them. They make a most wonderful gift to welcome a new friend to the world.

FINISHED MEASUREMENTS: APPROXIMATELY 8" (20CM) TALL

materials

1 piece organic cotton flannel or cotton color-grown fleece fabric, approximately 18" x 12" (46x30.5cm)

1 circle medium-weight organic cotton interlock fabric, approximately 6" (15cm) in diameter

Organic cotton batting for stuffing (All organic cotton used here is from Organic Cotton Plus)

Lightweight scrap cotton cloth approximately 6" (15cm) square

notions

Paper for making patterns

Scissors

Matching sewing thread and hand sewing needle

Beeswax crayon in red or pink

Non-toxic acrylic paint in desired eye color and in red for mouth

Straight pins

sewing techniques

Simple running stitch (see page 141)

TEMPLATE PAGE 122

TIPS *If you choose to use embroidery to create the doll's face (instead of painting on a face), stitch the face BEFORE sewing on the hat so you can tie off and knot the ends of the embroidery thread to the back of the head, and then hide the knots under the hat.*

starting out

Wad together cotton batting until a very solid ball slightly larger than a golf ball has formed. This will be the head. As you make more dolls, determine just what size head you prefer. Take the piece of scrap cloth and place the cotton "ball" in its center. Pull the bottom edges down tight as if wrapping the cotton ball. Then, with threaded needle, gather the raw edges of the fabric and secure the cloth around the cotton ball.

Next, place the circle of cotton interlock (sometimes referred to as "stockinette") over the head. Gather the edges of the circle under the head and begin to tighten. You want to keep one side of the head very smooth; the other side will be under a hat. Gather the interlock tightly under the head and smooth the wrinkles to the back side of the head where you can stitch them into place. Once you have a round, firmly covered head with one nice, smooth side, gather and securely sew the lower edge together and proceed to the body.

making the doll's body

With the fabric of your choice, cut your 12" x 18" (30x46cm) piece. Fold this piece twice into rough quarters, placing the right sides facing each other as you fold. Enlarge the body and hat pieces 25%. Trace the patterns onto paper, and cut out for pattern pieces. Lay the body pattern onto the folded cloth with marked dashed lines along folds of fabric. Orient the pattern at the upper left corner, with the center of the body at the center fold and the shoulder meeting the double-thick fold. Pin into place and cut out the body piece. Then, cut the small section at the top left for the neck opening.

Open the folded cloth to reveal the doll's body, ready to sew with right sides together. Following the dotted lines on the pattern for seam allowance, sew around the body, leaving an opening between the legs for stuffing later. If you are using knit or fine fabric, you may wish to machine sew, though hand-sewing is a lovely way to make these dolls. Once you have completed the sewing, turn the doll right-side out.

From your scraps, use one of the tall round pieces remaining from the area under the arm and over the leg for the hat. Fold this piece in half, and lay the tracing of the hat pattern onto it, aligning the center at the fold; cut around the pattern piece. Sew the hat up the center back. Turn right-side out.

Next, take the needle and sewing thread and make a small running stitch all the way around the neck opening, a little less than $1/4$" (.6cm) below the raw edge. If you tighten this slightly, you will find it coaxes the fabric to fold into the inside of the doll's neck. Then, place the head in this opening, lowering it all the way down so all the raw edges and securing stitches of the "neck" are well inside the body. Now, carefully align the doll's head with the back of the head toward the back of the body and the front to the front; take tiny stitches by hand to invisibly sew the folded-in neck edge to the base of the doll's head, using small, even, and careful stitches.

Place the hat on the head, covering up all the wrinkles and what-have-yous on the back of the head. The lower edge of the hat should be turned under—this can usually be done by a simple finger pressing. The seam is in back, and the back base of the hat should meet up with the body of the doll. Stitch the back of the hat to the back "neckline" of the doll. Then, carefully and invisibly stitch the hat around the doll's head. You may play around with the angle of the hat to achieve different results and expressions.

making the hands and legs

Knots will form the doll's hands and legs. To make these knots small and tight, start with large knots! For the first hand, begin to make the knot as if you were using up the whole arm, and the knot was going to be at the shoulder. Keep it loose. Then, gently coax the knot down the length of the arm until it is at the desired hand location. When it is in just the right spot, push and pull it to make it very tight. Repeat this for the other arm and on the legs for the feet.

stuffing

Lightly stuff the doll with organic cotton batting, or should you prefer, no stuffing at all. You may wish to place a few drops of calming lavender essential oil on the cotton stuffing; this is a nice touch as well. Once the doll is stuffed to the desired result, invisibly hand-sew the opening at the legs closed.

decorating

Using nontoxic acrylic paint, very carefully apply the most simple of faces to the doll. I use a darning needle or a slender double-pointed knitting needle to dab little dots for the eyes, and a really tiny, thin paintbrush to apply the mouth. If you would like to make the doll entirely from fiber, consider embroidering the face with two simple stitches for the eyes and one longer running stitch for the mouth, in desired colors of embroidery floss. If you are using paint, let the paint completely dry before you touch the doll. It is heartbreaking to accidentally smear a beautiful face. If you like, apply rosy cheeks by lightly rubbing a beeswax crayon against the cheeks. Very detailed instructions on making dolls' faces can be found in the doll-making titles listed in the "For Further Reading" section, and I highly recommend taking a look at them if you have enjoyed this project!

The Nature of Play and Toys from Nature

Kids and babies play—it's what they do. In fact, I've heard it said several times that for children, play is their work. In essence, it is through active play that children learn social skills and develop their capacities for cooperation and empathy. Play is crucial for the development of problem-solving skills and self-confidence, and it lays the groundwork for intellectual development and future academic success. These days, kids just don't play enough—in some schools, recess is being cut back or eliminated altogether.

Throughout a child's developmental stages, unstructured, imaginative play is one of the most important activities in which our kids can engage. Have you seen how many ways a little boy can find sticks and a rock fascinating? Take it from me: I continue to find rocks in my third-grader's pockets, and my two-year-old is now carrying on the tradition with an extensive collection of sticks, each of which seems to have a unique function.

Imaginative play stimulates the brain's creative centers and boosts intellectual development. It allows young children to explore their sensory and motor skills, enhancing physical well-being. It also encourages our kids to connect with the world and with nature in magical ways. Imagination, fantasy, and creative play foster a life-long love of learning, helping our kids to grow into insightful, confident adults and happy people.

In early childhood, we can start our babies' love of play off in the right direction by providing them with lovely playthings handcrafted from natural materials. Natural materials in particular encourage children to develop their tactile senses and provide them with a connection to the natural world around them. Babies especially need toys that provide them with representations of the beauty of the world.

Materials that come from nature possess warmth, texture, and organic unique-ness that encourage touch, manipulation, and interaction. Interaction with tac-tile elements like soft cloth, warm wood, and gentle colors supports the development of fine motor skills and, in turn, enhances concentration and focus. Young children are invited to explore and develop their senses and awaken their innate creativity. Not only does a simple toy reinforce an appre-ciation for nature, but it also invites appreciation for natural materials and artistry.

Simple, natural toys—those without batteries and flashing lights—engage a child's imagination on multiple levels. The less complex the toy, the more pos-sibilities exist for the child to come up with imaginative ways to use it. A sim-ple doll can be a comforting, soft item in infancy, a companion in babyhood, and a baby to play house with later in childhood. A block can be a car, a build-ing material, or a thing to play toss with or hurl around. Additionally, the simplicity of such toys allows for extended periods of imaginative play, thus increasing a child's ability to concentrate and engage successfully in individu-ally directed tasks and improving attention spans.

In place of the plastic, disposable, single-use toys that are so abundant these days, simple, natural toys absorb the child in a world of touch and fantasy. Rather than perpetuating the culture of a disposable society, handmade toys allow for a child's relationship with nature to expand—something that seems to be getting lost in the fray of modern life. Combined with creative and imagina-tive play, these toys help lay the foundation for our little ones to develop a strong sense of the natural world and their place in it.

flannel star babies

An adorable and easy-to-make project, the little star baby is also a classic handwork baby doll. Made from all-natural materials, it is cut from organic cotton flannel and stuffed with organic cotton batting.

FINISHED MEASUREMENTS: APPROXIMATELY 6" (15.2CM) TALL

materials

7" x 9" (18x23cm) piece of organic flannel in yellow

4" (10cm) square organic cotton interlock

Organic cotton batting for stuffing

4" (10cm) square scrap fabric for inner lining of head

(Organic cotton materials shown here are from Organic Cotton Plus)

notions

Paper for making patterns

Hand-sewing needle and sewing thread

Non-toxic acrylic paint and very small paintbrush OR embroidery thread and needle in desired eye color and red for mouth (red optional)

Red beeswax crayon

Straight pins

sewing techniques (optional)

Embroidery stitches: French knots (see page 141), single running stitch (see page 141)

TEMPLATE PAGE 123

TIPS If you choose to use embroidery to create the doll's face (instead of painting on a face), stitch the face BEFORE sewing on the hat so you can tie off and knot the ends of the embroidery thread to the back of the head, and then hide the knots under the hat.

starting out

Make the head first: Wad together cotton batting until a very solid ball approximately 1" (2.5cm) in diameter has formed. As you make more dolls, you will determine just what size you prefer. Take the piece of scrap cloth, and place the cotton "ball" in its center. Pull the bottom edges down tight as if wrapping the cotton ball. Then, with threaded needle, gather the raw edges of the fabric and secure the cloth under the cotton ball.

Then, trace the pattern for the body and hat onto paper, and cut out to create a paper pattern.

making the star baby

Fold the flannel in quarters. Following layout instructions on pattern piece, place the top and center of pattern piece along folds. Cut out entire body (front and back) all in one piece from cotton flannel. If you would like to add any embellishment, embroidery, or monograms, now is the time. If your baby is going to be plain, proceed to the next step.

Sew around the body, leaving an opening to insert stuffing between the legs. Turn the piece right-side out. Lightly stuff with a small bit of batting, just to give the baby a little puffy shape. Invisibly stitch the opening for the stuffing closed. With needle and thread, make a running basting stitch around the head opening. Cut the thread, leaving long enough ends to pull tight later.

Next, place the circle of cotton interlock (sometimes referred to as "stockinette") over the head. Gather the edges of the circle under the head and begin to tighten. You want to keep one side of the head very smooth; the other side will be under a hat. Gather the interlock tightly under the head, and smooth the wrinkles to the back side of the head where you can stitch them into place. Once you have a round, firmly covered head with one nice smooth side, gather and securely sew the lower edges together.

Insert the head into the head opening, finger pressing the raw edges to the inside. Make sure the smooth side of the head is facing forward. If you have embellished or decorated the baby, be sure the smooth side of the head is facing toward that side.

Gently pull on the basting thread around the head opening on the body to tighten around the neck. With needle and thread, take small, invisible stitches by hand around the base of the head through both thicknesses of flannel and into the interlock of the head. Stitch all the way around.

If you like, take tiny stitches a small way in from the end of each limb to define hands and feet, and knot top of hat if desired (as shown).

making the hat

Use the paper pattern to cut out the right fabric shape. Sew a single seam to join the sides of the hat. This seam denotes the back. Finger-press the raw edge of the hat up. Place the hat on the baby's head so that the back of the hat is pulled down to touch the body at the base of the neck and the front is well on the forehead. With needle and thread, take tiny and invisible stitches to sew the hat to the head, joining the hat to the flannel body at the back.

decorating

Using non-toxic acrylic paint, very carefully apply the most simple of faces to the doll. I use a darning needle or a slender double-pointed knitting needle to dab little dots for the eyes and a tiny paintbrush to apply the mouth. If you would like to make the doll entirely from fiber, consider embroidering the face with two simple stitches for the eyes and one longer running stitch for the mouth, in desired colors of embroidery floss. If you are using paint, let the paint completely dry before you touch the doll. It is heartbreaking to accidentally smear a beautiful face. If you like, apply rosy cheeks by lightly rubbing a beeswax crayon against the cheeks. Very detailed instructions on making doll's faces can be found in the doll-making titles listed in the "Techniques" section, and I highly recommend taking a look at them if you have enjoyed this project!

flower fairies

It is believed that magical play beginning at an early age stimulates the imagination and helps a child remain imaginative as he or she grows. In an age of satellite everything, information overload, and high-tech bombardment, imaginative play and development are crucial. These magical beings can be cut from felt or organic cotton and embellished as simply or as ornately as you like, or as the child's age dictates. These playful flower fairies touch upon a special place easily accessible to children (and some grownups, too). The use of natural elements and materials acclimates a child's senses to the richness and warmth available in the world. Please sew decorative elements on tightly to help prevent little fingers from pulling pieces loose. These delightful creatures may be best for older toddlers and young children, if you wish to keep their hair tidy and their wings intact and prevent bald spots!

FINISHED MEASUREMENTS: APPROXIMATELY 9" (23CM) TALL

materials

1 piece organic cotton flannel, approximately 10" x 18" (25x46cm) in natural for body

1 piece cotton broadcloth, approximately 10" x 2" (25x30cm), in slate blue or natural for fairy's dress

1 piece wool roving or clean fleece or organic cotton batting for stuffing

(Organic cotton materials shown here are from Organic Cotton Plus)

Materials for hair: carded wool roving, handful of mohair locks (can be found at most local yarn shops, at wool markets, or from online suppliers of handcrafting materials), or textured yarn

Recycled felt

notions

Paper and transfer or tracing paper for making patterns

Scissors

Hand-sewing needle and coordinating sewing thread (pieces may be sewn by hand or machine, as desired)

Sharp yarn needle

Red beeswax crayon

Ribbon roses (optional)

Silk flower petals (optional)

Non-toxic acrylic paint and very small paintbrush OR embroidery thread and needle in desired eye color and red for mouth (red optional)

sewing techniques

Embroidery stitches: satin stitch or French knots for embroidered eyes (see page 141), back stitch (see page 140), simple running stitch (see page 141)

TEMPLATE PAGE 124

making the body

Make a pattern for the doll body and dress by tracing the templates onto paper and cutting out the pattern pieces. Fold natural color organic flannel in half; using the pattern, cut two pieces for the body.

With RS facing, using matching thread, stitch the two pieces together (either by hand or machine), leaving an opening 1–2" (2.5–5cm) long to insert filling. Clip seams at corners and around head; turn the body right-side out. (If necessary, use a knitting needle or chopstick to turn piece fully.) Press piece lightly with a steam iron. Fill the body with stuffing to desired level of fullness. Using hand-sewing needle and matching thread, stitch the opening closed.

Next, cut out the dress pattern from paper as described above. Fold organic cotton broadcloth in half; using the pattern, cut two pieces for the dress. With right sides facing, using matching thread, stitch the shoulder and side seams together (either by hand or by machine) as follows:

Stitch from cuff to neck for each shoulder, and from lower edge to cuff on both sides. Clip seams as needed at corners, and turn right-side out. Press lightly, if necessary. Fold neck edge to inside approximately ¼" (.06cm); press and stitch in place. Repeat for cuffs.

Cut collar pattern from paper as described above. Using recycled felt, cut out collar. Place collar around neck of dress and seam at center back. If desired, tack in place around neck edge. Decorate collar and dress with ribbon roses or silk flower petals (as shown), and then dress the flower fairy by pulling her dress over her head.

decorating

Taking one piece of roving, wool, yarn, or mohair at a time, secure locks of hair around the base of the fairy's head, working up to the top; pay close attention to avoid "bald spots." A little goes a long way, so check your progress frequently, as it is easy to apply too much hair. To apply the locks, use needle and thread to sew a single back stitch and catch the lock in the back stitch before you tighten it down; continue in this manner around the head, applying in layers as necessary.

When you have worked all around the head, choose a special lock of hair or strand for the center front, and very carefully apply it at the center forehead at the hairline. Style hair if needed, but keep in mind that the more you mess with it, the messier it tends to look. After styling the hair, add ribbon roses or bows as desired. Secure the thread well and cut.

Use chalk or a light pencil dot to locate eye placement. Apply the fairy's eyes either by making eyes with two French knots in desired color of embroidery floss OR by painting two small dots in brown, black, or blue.

If painting, use a very small amount of paint mixed with an equal amount of water to create a liquid of gravy-like consistency. Using the paintbrush, simply touch the brush to the location of each eye, creating a nice, tiny round circle. Allow the paint to dry COMPLETELY before handling the doll again.

For cheek color, very lightly rub the tip of the red beeswax crayon at the location of the cheek, creating a soft pink glow.

About Organic Cotton

Truly organic cotton is grown without pesticides and is processed without chemicals like chlorine or formaldehyde. Organic cotton is grown free of toxic chemicals using biologically based, sustainable growing methods. Rather than using traditional twentieth-century agricultural practices, such as destructive fertilizers and chemical pesticides that contaminate and limit the health of soil, organic cotton is grown using systems such as crop rotation and biological pest control. These include the introduction of ladybugs as predator insects to maintain the health of the crop and the Earth.

For a long while it was thought that growing organic cotton was simply not feasible. Yet through the perseverance of dedicated farmers and the support of organic consumers, the production of organic cotton is becoming more and more mainstream. By adopting traditional and, in some cases, ancient growing methods, organic cotton products are now available to us in many forms, including yarns and fabrics. When we choose to use these materials, we support the businesses that diligently produce them, and we also support the stewardship of the Earth by putting our money into a burgeoning industry that does not corrupt the soil or introduce harsh chemicals and byproducts into the ecosystem.

wizard

This magical wizard inspires a special realm of creativity accessible to children. Sewn from all-organic cotton fabric and embellished with stars and mohair locks, this wise and fanciful wizard can open the door to hours of fun play and make an adorable decoration for children's rooms.
FINISHED SIZE: APPROXIMATELY 9" (22CM) TALL

materials

1 piece organic cotton flannel, approximately 10" x 18" (25x46cm), in Natural for body

1 piece cotton broadcloth, approximately 10" x 24" (25x61cm), in Slate Blue for robe and hat

Wool roving, clean fleece, or organic cotton batting for stuffing

(Organic cotton materials shown here are from Organic Cotton Plus)

Handful of mohair locks for hair and beard (can be found at most local yarn shops, at wool markets, or from on-line suppliers of handcrafting materials)

notions

Paper for making patterns
Scissors

Hand-sewing needle and coordinating sewing thread (pieces may be sewn by hand or machine, as desired)

Sharp yarn needle

Embroidery needle

Embroidery floss in yellow for stars and in eye color (optional, if you desire to embroider eyes)

Non-toxic child-safe water-based acrylic paint in eye color and size 0 paintbrush (optional, if you desire to paint eyes)

Red beeswax crayon

Straight pins

sewing techniques

Embroidery stitches: Simple running stitch (see page 141), back stitch, satin stitch or French knots for eyes (see pages 140–141)

TEMPLATE PAGES 124–125

making the body

Make a pattern for the doll body by tracing the templates onto paper and cutting out the pattern pieces. Fold natural color organic flannel in half; using the pattern, cut two pieces for the body.

With RS facing, using matching thread, stitch the two pieces together (either by hand or by machine), leaving an opening 1–2" (2.5–5cm) long to insert filling. Clip seams at corners and around head; turn the body right-side out. (If necessary, use a knitting needle or a chopstick to fully turn piece.) Press piece lightly with a steam iron. Fill the body with stuffing to desired level of fullness. Using hand-sewing needle and matching thread, stitch the opening closed.

making the robe

Enlarge and cut the robe pattern from paper. Fold blue broadcloth in half. Placing dashed line of pattern along fold, cut two pieces for robe. With RS facing, using matching thread, stitch the shoulder and side seams together, (either by hand or by machine) as follows: Stitch from cuff to neck for each shoulder, and from lower edge to cuff on both sides. Clip seams as needed at corners, and turn right-side out. Press lightly, if necessary. Fold neck edge to inside approximately ¼" (0.6cm); press and stitch in place. Repeat for cuffs.

decorating the robe

Using embroidery needle and yellow floss, stitch stars randomly on robe for decoration, using single stitches and back stitches as desired. Dress the wizard by pulling his robe over his head.

making the wizard hat

Enlarge and cut the hat pattern from paper. Cut one piece from blue broadcloth. With right sides facing, fold straight edges of hat together; sew along dotted line of straight seam and turn right-side out. Clip seam at point and lightly press seam, if necessary. Fold lower edge to inside approximately ¼" (0.6cm); press and stitch in place. Embellish with embroidered stars as for robe if desired.

applying the hair and beard

Taking one lock of mohair at a time, secure locks with small stitches and matching thread around the base of the wizard's head. You do not need to apply hair to his head where his hat will be—so you'll be leaving a "bald spot" over which his hat will be sewn.

To apply the locks, using thread and a hand-sewing needle, create a single back stitch and catch the lock in the back stitch before you tighten it down; continue in this manner around the head, applying two layers if necessary. Use this same technique to apply the beard, which will cover the mouth area. Place the hat on his head to see if any more mohair is needed for hair. Then, stitch the hat securely in place.

making the face

Use chalk or a light pencil dot to locate eye placement. Apply the wizard's eyes either by making eyes with two French knots in desired color of embroidery floss OR by painting two small dots in eye color. If painting, use a very small amount of paint mixed with an equal amount of water to create a liquid of gravy-like consistency. Using the paintbrush, simply touch the brush to the location of each eye, creating a nice, tiny round circle. Allow paint to dry COMPLETELY before handling the doll again. For cheek color, very lightly rub the tip of the red beeswax crayon at the location of the cheek, creating a soft pink glow if desired.

Finish your wizard's robe with a tie of wool roving. Then, go play!

angel-baby mobile

Every baby loves to gaze at shapes that move above them. Made from colorful and playful shapes that dangle from a piece of wood, this simple mobile can be used to decorate baby's room or a play area. Delightful little angels and simple star shapes are cut and sewn from felt, fiber, and roving. As they dangle and sway, each little angel releases blessings and spreads good will. The simplicity of the shapes, combined with a variety of colors and the gentle movement of the mobile, will keep baby engaged and happy! Consider creating variations of this project, making shapes from the templates provided in the other felt and handwork projects in this collection. Please note that the mobile should never hang directly over the crib, or within reach of baby.

SIZE: WILL VARY DEPENDING ON YOUR MOOD AND MATERIALS.
FINISHED MEASUREMENTS: (AS SHOWN) APPROXIMATELY 18" (46CM) WIDE WITH FOUR ANGELS AND FIVE STARS

materials

Felt: Assortment of recycled felt in various colors for angels, enough for five stars in one color (or assorted colors if you wish), plus small pieces for angel wings (shown in various colors)

1 piece of organic cotton interlock, approximately 12" x 12" (30x30cm) for heads

(Organic cotton materials shown here are from Organic Cotton Plus)

Embroidery needle and embroidery floss for eyes in desired colors

Embroidery thread for hanging pieces of the mobile (gold metallic shown)

Wool locks, wool roving, or organic cotton batting to stuff heads

Wool roving or mohair locks for hair

Stick or wooden dowel approximately 18" (46cm) long

notions

Paper for making patterns
Scissors
Hand-sewing needle and thread
Red beeswax crayon
Length of yarn or cord for hanging
Beeswax (optional)
Glue (optional)

sewing techniques

Hand embroidery: Simple hand-sewn running stitch (see page 141), single stitch or French knot for eyes (see page 141)

TEMPLATE PAGE 126

making the angels

Make a pattern by tracing the angel template onto paper. Place pattern on felt as instructed and cut out the desired number of bodies. Cut a small "X" at the top center of the angel body on fold at the location of the head on each body piece.

Use paper pattern to make the heads. Place pattern on organic cotton as instructed on the piece and cut out required number of circular heads. Using the stuffing of choice, wad up a small bit and place it in the center of the circle. Using needle and thread, gather up the outside edges of the circle, creating one side that is smooth. Secure the head and base of the head at the neck edge with small stitches.

Next, attach the head to the body by dropping the needle through the small "X" shaped opening, and then poking the base of the head through to the inside. On the inside, take tiny stitches and secure the head to the body at neck. Then, again with small stitches, tack the body closed at each underarm. Secure and cut thread. Repeat for each angel.

decorating

Embellish each face with rosy cheeks by gently rubbing red beeswax crayon at the location of each cheek. Mark the location of the eyes lightly in pencil. Then, with embroidery needle threaded with floss, poke needle up on the inside through the base of the head to the marked location. Make two tiny stitches or small French knots for the eyes; secure the thread and cut.

stitching hair onto head

To create the hair, thread the sewing needle with a color coordinating with the fiber chosen for the hair. Using wool roving or mohair locks, take small pieces, one at a time, and secure the fiber at the center of each lock, letting the hair hang—half on each side of your stitch. Do this around the head, paying close attention to avoid "bald spots." A little goes a long way, so check your progress frequently, as it is easy to apply too much hair.

When you have worked all around the head, choose a special lock or strand for the center front and very carefully apply it at the center forehead at the hair-line. Style hair if needed, but keep in mind the more you mess with it, the messier it tends to look. Secure the thread and cut.

applying angel wings

Give the angels wings, either one color, or many different colors (as shown). You might even choose different materials for each set of wings, such as leaves from silk flowers or feathers. To make the felt wings, simply trace the wing pattern templates onto felt or the fabric of your choice and cut out the set. With sewing needle and coordinating thread, stitch the wings to the angel's back. To make the wings stand up a bit, fold them together and make a couple of tiny stitches through both thicknesses at the base of the wings (optional). Repeat for each angel.

To make stars, using the paper pattern template, trace the star shape onto felt and cut out the desired number of stars.

assembling the mobile

If you have chosen to use a stick or a branch, wipe the wood well to clean off dirt. For a light sheen, consider polishing the stick (beeswax works well). Lay out pieces to be suspended in the order you wish to hang them. On mobile shown, stars alternate with angels. You could also include hearts or moons instead.

Using the chosen thread, attach one end of the thread to the first piece to be hung. Determine how far down you want the piece to hang and then tie the thread around the stick or dowel, knotting well; cut end. Repeat for each angel and star, suspending them at different heights for interest.

Be aware that the closer together the pieces are placed, the more easily they will tangle together. When finished, consider a dab of glue at the location of each knot on the wood to secure the thread in place. Use a strand of strong yarn, cord, ribbon, or other strong material to create a hanger by attaching it to each end of the wood. Again, a dab of glue will further secure the hanger. Hang from the ceiling or door frame, well out of reach from baby.

sherpa fleece pants and jacket set

These organic cotton Sherpa fleece garments are fashioned from the simplest of shapes and can be assembled and sewn by even a beginning sewer. A few straight seams, a couple of hems, and voila! The softness and organic qualities of this lovely fleece cuddle your baby in warmth. A loving gift for your own child or someone else's, this project can be worked up quickly by a veteran seamstress or can act as a delightful introduction to garment making for a novice stitcher. Because the set is assembled much like a sweater, the process will be familiar to a knitter.

SIZE: 12 MONTHS (FOR INSTRUCTIONS ON ADAPTING SIZE, SEE BELOW)

NOTE *To make larger or smaller size, measure a sweater and/or leggings that fit baby well, allowing for ease and a bit for growing. Use these measurements to cut out your pieces, following shapes given.*

materials

1 yd (1m) organic cotton sherpa fleece
(Organic cotton materials shown here are from Organic Cotton Plus)
Hand-sewing needle and coordinating thread
Five $3/8"$ (.94cm) buttons
1 package of single-fold bias tape in coordinating color
Approximately 1 yd (1m) of $1/2"$ or 1" (1.25 or 2.5cm) waistband elastic
Sewing machine, if desired

notions

Paper for making patterns
Scissors
Straight pins

NOTE *For best results, use a sewing machine.*

TEMPLATE PAGE 128

starting out

Make a pattern for pants and jacket pieces by copying and enlarging the templates onto paper. Cut out the pattern pieces. Wash and dry the cotton fleece fabric.

Cut out four pieces of fleece from pants pattern piece.

making the pants

Place fabric pieces right sides facing to create two sets-one for the front of the pants, one for the back. Sew center front and back seams; edge stitch or zigzag close to seam and trim excess.

Open front and back sections; place right sides together, matching top edges and stitch lines. Sew side seams.
Sew inseam from cuff to cuff; edge stitch or zigzag close to seam and trim excess.

Finish the cuffs as follows: First zigzag around cuff edge. Press up 1" (2.5cm), or desired length, and stitch hem around lower leg. Repeat for other side.

Create a waistband/elastic casing by zigzag stitching around top edge of pants. Fold and press top edge down approximately 1¼" (3.2cm). Stitch in place, leaving approximately 2" (5cm) opening to insert elastic. Next, measure length of elastic needed from the waistband of a pair of pants that comfortably fits the baby, or by wrapping elastic loosely around baby's waist with no stretch and add a little extra ease; cut to

desired length. Thread elastic through the waistband/add casing, beginning and ending at the 2" (5cm) opening, making sure you secure the ends so they don't pull through as you tug on the elastic. Overlap the elastic slightly and securely sew together. Sew the 2" (5cm) opening shut.

making the jacket

Cut out pieces of fleece from jacket pattern pieces as indicated on pattern pieces.

With RS facing each other, sew shoulder seams; edge stitch or zigzag close to seam and trim excess.

Pin sleeves in place between notches as indicated on pattern piece. Stitch in place; edge stitch or zigzag close to seam. Trim the excess, leaving side seam selvedge intact.

Pin side/underarm seams, matching lower edges, cuff, and underarm seams. Stitch edge; edge stitch or zigzag close to seam and trim excess.

Zigzag stitch across bottom edge and around the cuffs of the jacket all the way around and press up a 1"- (2.5cm-) wide hem, then stitch the hem in place. Use the same technique to make the cuff hems, turning up 1" (2.5cm) of fabric and stitching up hem.

To finish the neck, use bias tape as neck facing. Open out one edge of bias tape and pin to neck edge, with right sides together. Cut to necessary length. Sew seam, turn bias tape to inside, lightly press, and stitch in place.

front bands

Cut length of bias tape to match length of front edges. Pin to edges, with right sides together, as a front band facing. Sew seam, trim as needed, turn bias tape to inside, lightly press, and stitch in place.

buttonholes

NOTE *Alternate closures such as frogs or toggles may be used instead.*

Mark location of five buttons on desired side (buttonholes are on the left front for boys/unisex, on the right front for girls). Make corresponding ½" (1.25cm) buttonholes on opposite side using your sewing machine's buttonhole feature. Sew buttons very securely in place on opposite front.

Trim all stray threads. If desired, wash and dry garment before initial wearing.

templates

The following templates accompany the projects from the felting and sewing chapters. To create a pattern from a template, simply trace the template onto a piece of paper and, where indicated, enlarge using a photocopier.

truck appliqué template recycled wool toddler jacket • page 64 • ENLARGE 50%

stitched moon and star toy templates stitched moon and stars toys • page 78 •
ENLARGE 50%

 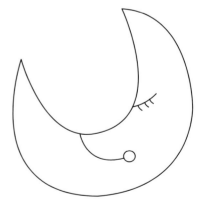

felt snake template
snuggly felt snake • page 80 • ENLARGE 25%

adjust length to fit length of your felt

center fold

lavender bear template
lavender-scented bear • page 86 • USE AT 100%

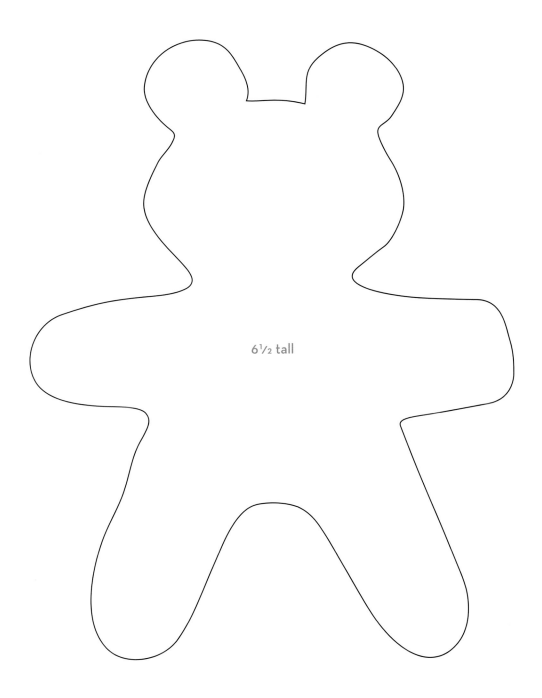

6½ tall

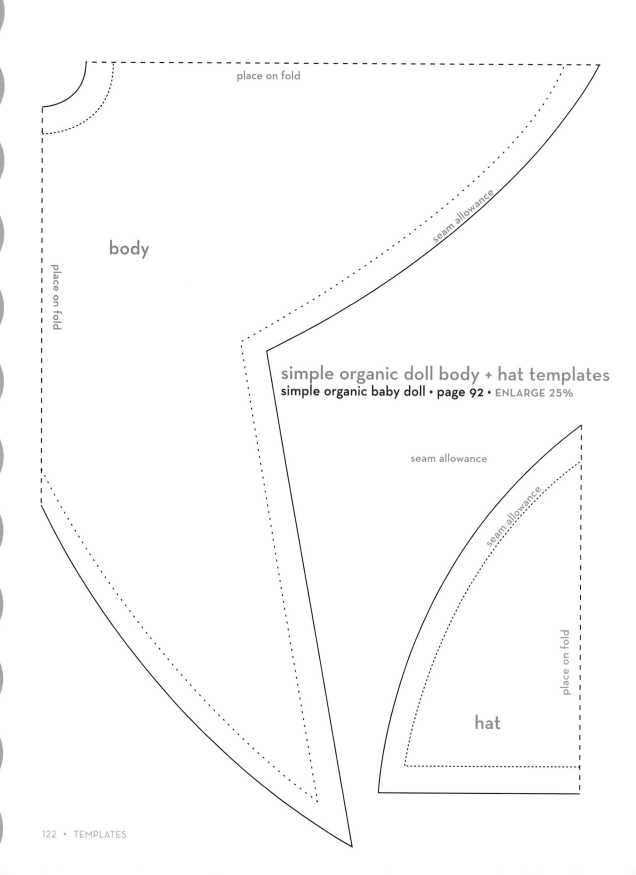

place on fold

body

place on fold

seam allowance

simple organic doll body + hat templates
simple organic baby doll • page 92 • ENLARGE 25%

seam allowance

seam allowance

place on fold

hat

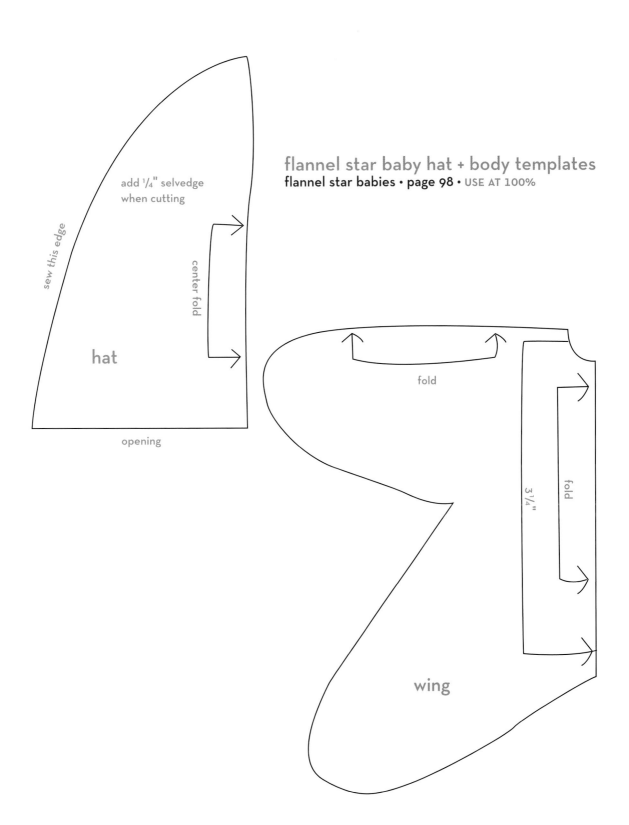

add ¼" selvedge when cutting

sew this edge

center fold

hat

opening

flannel star baby hat + body templates
flannel star babies • page 98 • USE AT 100%

fold

fold

3¼"

wing

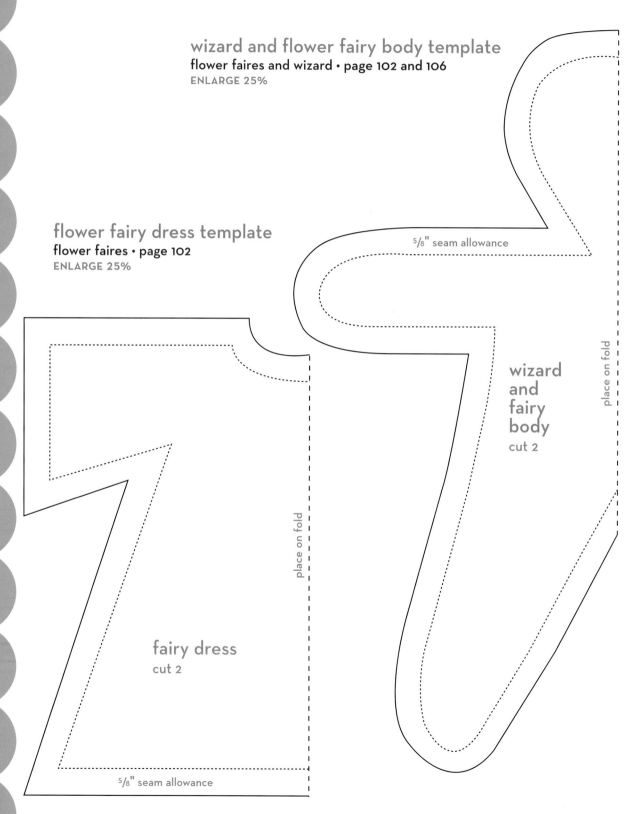

wizard and flower fairy body template
flower faires and wizard • page 102 and 106
ENLARGE 25%

flower fairy dress template
flower faires • page 102
ENLARGE 25%

⁵⁄₈" seam allowance

wizard
and
fairy
body

cut 2

place on fold

place on fold

fairy dress

cut 2

⁵⁄₈" seam allowance

wizard robe and hat templates
wizard • page 106
ENLARGE 25%

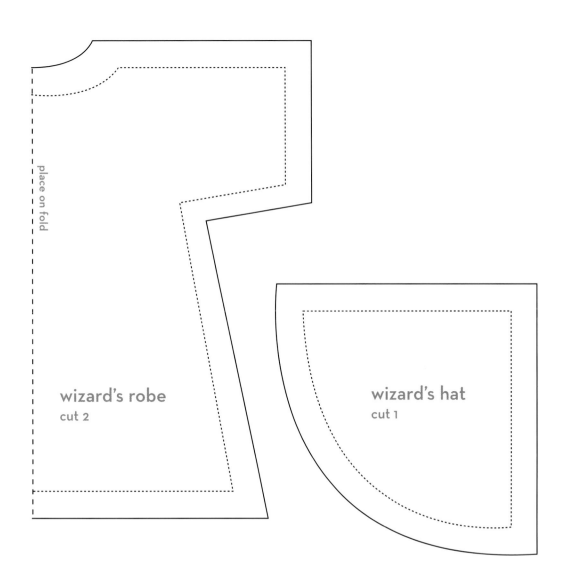

place on fold

wizard's robe
cut 2

wizard's hat
cut 1

angel–baby mobile templates **angel–baby mobile** • page 110 • USE AT 100%

top

felt star 3" wide

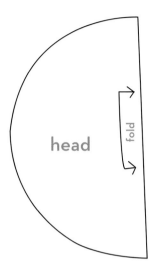

head

fold

cut from cotton (on fold) 7³/₄ diameter

wings

fold

cut from felt (on fold) 1³/₄–2" wide

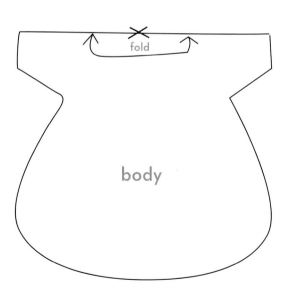

fold

body

cut from felt (on fold) 2¹/₄" squared

hot-water bottle cover

sherpa fleece pants and jacket templates
sherpa fleece pants and jacket • page 114 • ENLARGE 50%

jacket front
cut 2

5/8" seam allowance

5/8" seam allowance

sleeve
cut 2

place on fold

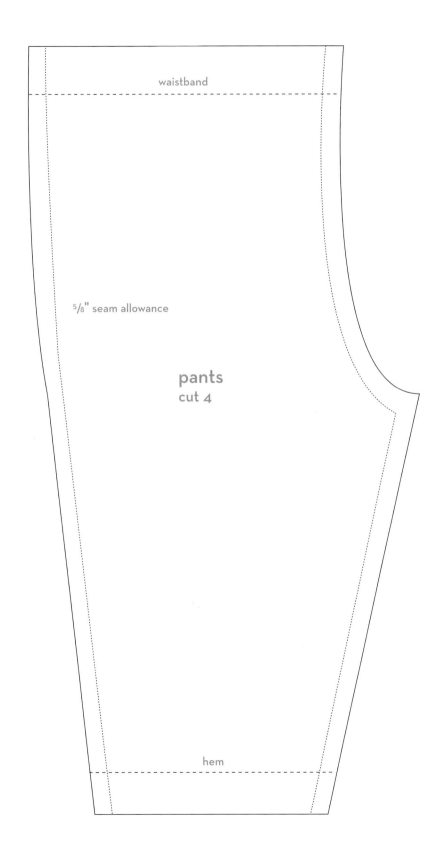

waistband

$^5/_8$" seam allowance

pants
cut 4

hem

circles–and–squares hat 9-18 months • **page 68** • ENLARGE 50%

top knot hat 9-18 months • **page 70** • ENLARGE 50%

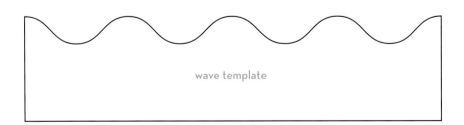

wave template

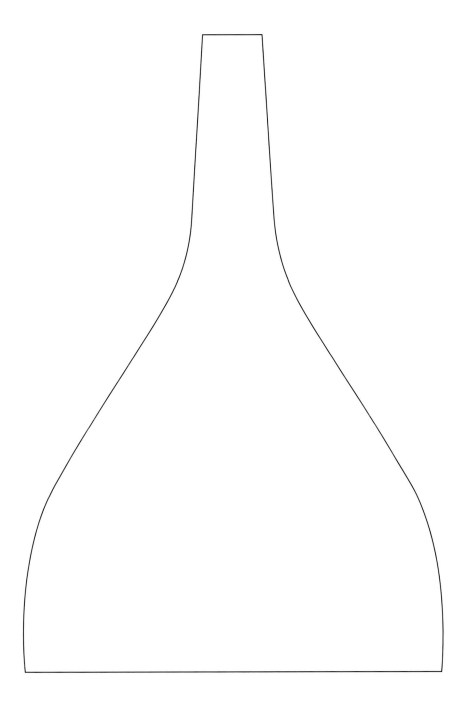

daisy hat 9-18 months • **page 72** • ENLARGE 50%

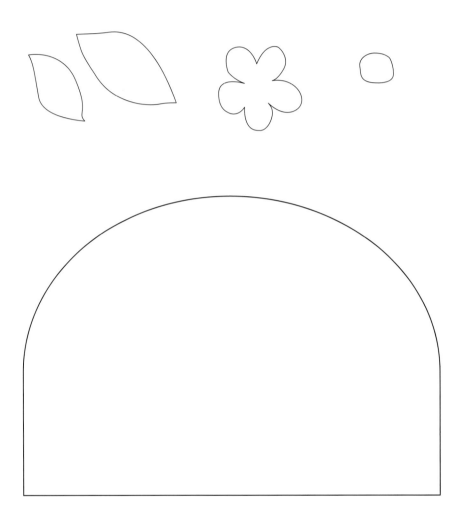

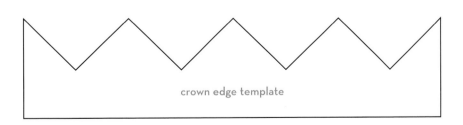

crown edge template

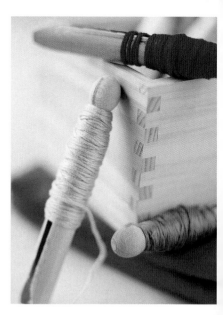

techniques guide

Each project in *Nature Babies* includes a section highlighting the knitting, sewing, or embroidery techniques used in that pattern. In this guide you will find instructions and illustrations for some of the key techniques—some of these I have included because they appear throughout the book, others because they are less commonplace. Whether these skills are new to you, or you simply need a quick reminder, I hope you will find the guides an invaluable resource as you craft the projects in *Nature Babies*.

knitting techniques

buttonholes

A technique that entails placing holes or breaks in the fabric to accommodate button closures.

There are two common methods for making buttonholes, the two-row buttonhole and the yarn-over buttonhole (instructions for both follow). Both are easy to do. The two-row buttonhole gives a more finished look and is completed in two steps. The yarn-over buttonhole simply makes a hole in the fabric and can be completed in just one step. The individual patterns include details on buttonhole placement, but the standard location for buttonholes on girls' garments is the right-hand side (when worn) and for boys' and unisex garments on the left-hand side.

two row buttonhole (worked over two rows)

Row 1: Work to desired location of buttonhole. BO 1 or 2 stitches as directed, continue to work even across row. (Illus. A)

Row 2: Work as established to the gap created by the bound off stitches. Loosely CO 1 or 2 stitches (the same number you bound off) over the gap. (Illus B)

Continue to work even across row.

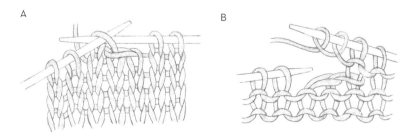

A   B

yarn-over buttonhole

Knit to the location of your buttonhole, make a yarn over, then knit the next two stitches together. On the next row, simply work as usual in the established pattern.

tip *First, knit the front that will not have buttonholes. Then, before you work the other side, mark the button locations on the first front with contrasting yarn or safety pins. Do this by either measuring or eyeballing it. When you make the front that has buttonholes, as you knit, measure it against the front with the markers. When you reach the approximate location of each marker, it's time to make a buttonhole. Continue in this manner until all the buttonholes have been completed.*

decrease (dec)

A method for reducing the number of stitches on your needle. Also a technique for manipulating the shape of the knitted piece, such as when making a neck opening rounded or a sleeve tapered. The two most common decreasing methods used in this book are knit two together (k2tog) and slip slip knit (SSK).

knit two together (k2tog)

The most straightforward and common method of decreasing. To do this, insert the tip of the right-hand needle into the first two stitches on the left-hand needle as if they were one. (Illus. A) Then pull the new stitch through the two old stitches and let the old stitches both fall off the left-hand needle. (Illus. B) This decrease makes the stitches lean toward the right. (Illus. C) You can also purl two together on the wrong side or if you are working in stockinette stitch.

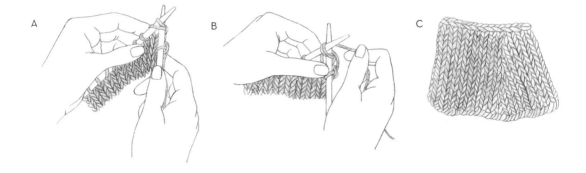

A   B   C

slip slip knit (SSK)

Slip the next two stitches from the left-hand needle as if to knit onto the right-hand needle. (Illus. A) Then , insert the left-hand needle through the front of the slipped stitches (Illus. B) and knit them together. (Illus. C) This method of decreasing makes the stitches lean toward the left.

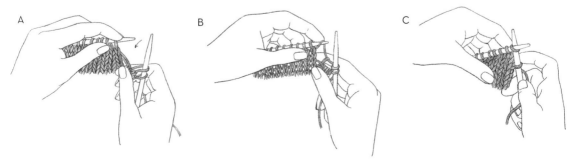

A   B   C

increase

In this book, the make one (M1) method of adding new stitches is used to introduce a new, nearly invisible stitch into the established knitted fabric to shape your knitting or make it wider.

make one (M1)

When you have reached the location of the increase, insert the tip of the left-hand needle under the horizontal strand between the last and next stitches from back to front. (Illus. A) Lift the strand up and put it on the left-hand needle. (Illus. B) Knit into the back of this new "stitch." (Illus. C) If you are increasing at the beginning of a row, M1 after the first stitch. If at the end of a row, M1 before the last stitch of the row.

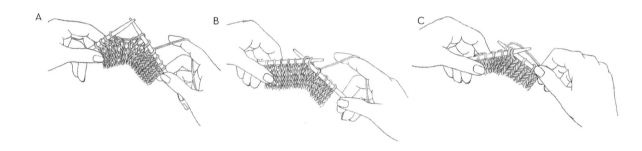

intarsia

A technique for knitting blocks of color using a different strand of each color for each color block worked.

In intarsia, instead of having many colors attached to lots of different balls of yarn, each color is often wound onto a bobbin and left to hang off the back of the piece until you work your way back and need the color again. Unlike stranded knitting, the style used to create a Nordic-style sweater, intarsia blocks are worked without carrying yarns behind the work. Rather, the yarn for each color used is isolated to the confines of its particular color block. When working an intarsia block of color, it is important to twist the two yarns together, locking them when you change from one color to the next so as not to knit a slit into your piece.

the basics of working intarsia

1. Cast on the specified number of stitches with yarn color A, and then cast on specified number of stitches with yarn color B. (Illus. A)
2. Knit across the stitches of yarn color B, and then pick up color A and bring it under color B. (Illus. B)

3. Next, knit the stitches in color A. Repeat steps 2 and 3 across the row as many times as needed, interlocking yarns at transition points. (Illus. C)
4. For the purl row, purl across stitches in color B, drop B, pick up A and bring it up under color B, and purl across stitches in color A.

A   B   C

knit two together (k2tog)

See Decreasing.

make one (m1)

See Increasing.

three-needle bind-off

A join that produces what looks like a perfect seam using three needles—two that hold the live stitches of the pieces to be joined and a third used to work the bind-off. A great way to join two pieces of knitting without sewing a seam, this technique is almost identical to that of a standard bind-off and is sometimes referred to as *binding off two pieces together*.

Place stitches from holders onto two needles with right sides facing and the tips of both needles pointing in the same direction. Be sure to match the left shoulder front to the left shoulder back and the right front to the right back.

Hold these two needles parallel in your left hand so they both act as the left-hand needle. Insert a third needle (used as the right-hand needle) through the first stitch on the front needle, and then the first stitch on the back needle. Knit the two stitches together as one, and slide them both off the needles. Repeat, creating a second stitch on the right-hand needle.

Then, perform the first bind-off by slipping the first stitch worked over the second stitch worked and off the needle. Repeat the process until all stitches are bound off. Cut the yarn, leaving a 12" (28cm) tail and draw tail through the remaining loop. Weave in the end.

embroidery and sewing techniques

appliqué

appliqué

An embellishment technique in which a motif cut from separate pieces of cloth or fabric is applied to a garment or larger piece of fabric for decoration.

Cut your appliqué motif pieces and position as you like onto the garment or fabric. Pin in place and then sew using invisible or decorative stitching, such as blanket/buttonhole stitch or whipstitch, around the edges of the motif.

backstitch

backstitch

A technique used to create an outline stitch or to hold appliqué motifs in place.

Working from right to left, as shown, make a row of small stitches, inserting the needle into the end of the previous stitch each time.

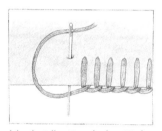

blanket/button hole stitch

blanket/buttonhole stitch

A simple, decorative finish for projects and a round appliqué piece. When using felt, the raw edges need not be turned or pressed under.

Bring the thread up just above the fabric edge, as shown.
Then take the needle down through the fabric and loop the thread around the needle where it emerges at the edge.

chain stitch

chain stitch

A simple stitch that creates a linked row of interlocking loops, chain stitch is made by looping the thread under the needle as you pull it through the fabric. Begin the next chain stitch by inserting the needle where it last emerged.

duplicate stitch

A form of embroidery that simulates two-color knitting by sewing over a knitted stitch using knit stitch with a new color.

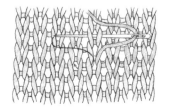

duplicate stitch

french knot

Little stitches that sit slightly raised above the work.

To make a French knot, pull the thread through the fabric and then, hold-ing the thread slightly taut with your thumb, twist the needle around twice. Insert the needle back through the fabric at the starting point and pull it through to create a knot.

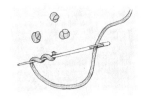

french knot

lazy daisy stitch

Also known as detached chain stitch. Very similar to chain stitch.

In lazy daisy, each stitch stands alone, anchored by a stitch at the top of the loop.

lazy daisy stitch

satin stitch

A smooth stitch that works well for edging or filling in embroidered forms. Looks best worked with shiny thread.

Work stitches all in the same direction, as shown, placed neatly and even-ly side by side.

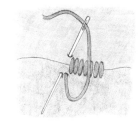

satin stitch

simple running stitch

A good outline stitch, especially when worked in a contrasting color to the background fabric.

The size of running stitch can be changed to match the scale of the proj-ect, but it is essential to keep the stitches equal and evenly spaced. The running stitch can also be used to sew pieces of fabric together in hand sewing. When used this way, stitches should be small and closely spaced.

simple running stitch

whipstitch

A technique that helps keep appliqué from fraying at the edge. Also used to create an almost invisible seam.

Each stitch in whipstitch overlaps the last and reinforces the edge being stitched.

whipstitch

yarn substituton

For the knitting projects in this book, I recommend that you use the yarns specified. However, if you would like to make a substitution, make sure your selection is as close as possible to the yarn suggested in thickness, weight, and texture. Determine the amount that you will need by yards/meters rather than by weight. You can find yarn weights listed on the label or on the website provided in the Suppliers list, but if you're unsure about substitution, try knitting a gauge swatch—it should match. The gauge and recommended needle size on the yarn label will help indicate the yarn thickness.

suppliers

All of the projects in this book call for materials that are readily available at yarn and craft stores near you. The list below will help you find organic materials to complete the projects. If you have trouble finding a product at the stores in your area, consult the websites listed to locate a distributor near you.

yarn and materials

Blue Sky Alpacas
www.blueskyalpacas.com
888-460-8862
sylvia@blueskyalpacas.com

Botanical Shades
413-625-9492
botanicalshades@comcast.net

Dancing Fibers
Distributor of Pakucho Organic Cloth
www.dancingfibers.com
806-797-3332
yarn@dancingfibers.com

EnviroTextiles
www.envirotextile.com/hemp-yarns.htm
970-945-5986
info@envirotextile.com

foamonline.com
805-964-2001
info@foamonline.com

Green Mountain Spinnery
www.spinnery.com
800-321-9665
spinnery@sover.net

Manos del Uruguay
Distributed by Design Source
888-566-9970
shangold@aol.com

Mostly Merino
802-254-7436
info@mostlymerino.com

Near Sea Naturals
www.nearseanaturals.com
info@nearseanaturals.com

Organic Cotton Plus
www.organiccottonplus.com
866-784-0374
info@organiccottonplus.com

Vreseis Limited
www.vreseis.com
530-796-3007
info@vreseis.com

wool felt

A Child's Dream Come True
www.achildsdream.com
800-359-2906
info@achildsdream.com

The Felt People
www.thefeltpeople.com
800-631-8968

La Lana Wools
www.lalanawools.com
505-758-9631 (info)
888-377-9631 (orders)
lalana@lalanawools.com

mohair locks (dyed and undyed)

Kai Ranch Mohair
www.kairanch.com
shell@kairanch.com
512-273-2709

for further reading

Alliance for Childhood. *Time for Play, Everyday.* www.allianceforchildhood.org

Cooper, Stephanie, et al. *The Children's Year.* Gloucestershire: Hawthorn Press, 1986.

Editors of Readers Digest. *New Complete Guide to Sewing.* Pleasantville, NY: Readers Digest Books, 2002.

Editors of Vogue Knitting. *Vogue Knitting: The Ultimate Knitting Book.* New York: Sixth and Spring Books, 2002.

Emerson, Jayne and Docherty, Margaret. *Simply Felt: 20 Easy and Elegant Designs in Wool.* Loveland, CO: Interweave Press, 2004.

Heath, Alan & Bainbridge, Nicki. *Baby Massage: The Calming Power of Touch.* New York: DK Adult Books, 2004.

Iannaccone, Carmine. "History, Humanity and Handwork." *Renewal: Journal of the Association of Waldorf Schools of North America, Fall/Winter 2001.* Fair Oaks, CA: Association of Waldorf Schools of North America (AWSNA).

McClure, Vimala. *Infant Massage: A Handbook for Loving Parents.* New York: Bantam: 2000.

Reincken, Sunnhild. *Making Dolls.* Edinburgh: Floris Books, 1990.

Sealey, Maricristin. *Kinder Dolls: A Waldorf Doll-Making Handbook.* Gloucestershire: Hawthorn Press, 2001.

Trosstli, Roberto. *Rhythms of Learning.* Great Barrington, MA: Steiner Books/Anthroposophical Press, 1998.

Vickrey, Anne. *The Art of Feltmaking: Basic Techniques for Making Jewelry, Miniatures, Dolls, Buttons, Wearables, Puppets, Masks and Fine Art Pieces.* New York: Watson-Guptill Publications, 1997.

Wilson, Roberta. *Aromatherapy: Essential Oils for Vibrant Health and Beauty.* New York, Avery: 2002.

of interest

The Organic Trade Association
www.ota.com
The Organic Trade Association (OTA) is a business association that promotes organic products and helps set industry standards in North America.

The O' Mama Report
www.theorganicreport.com
info@theorganicreport.org
The OTA has created this online resource for women who want to make informed decisions about organic agriculture and other organic products. The website serves as a platform for women to share their ideas, experiences, and sources of inspiration.

National Association for Holistic Aromatherapy
www.naha.org
info@naha.org
The National Association for Holistic Aromatherapy is a nonprofit organization that specializes in increasing public awareness of and setting educational standards for aromatherapy.

acknowledgments

Thanks to my nature babies, Jack and Zane. Thanks to Bill—I love you. Thanks to all the suppliers and manufacturers who have provided materials for this very special project. Thanks to Diane Carlson for her speedy needles and knitting expertise. Thanks to Jamie Little for her nimble fingers and open heart. Thanks to Linda Roghaar for everything and to the fantastic folks at Potter Craft. Thanks to Carole Summer and Jill Jones for their expert knowledge. Thanks to the supporters and producers of small batch, natural, and organic materials and products, who have persevered and helped to "close the gap." Thanks to the dedicated practitioners of handwork and holistic arts and their commitment to an enlightened society. Thanks to all the little ones in our lives who inspire us to do more, do better, and keep the world beautiful.

index